DISCARDED

DATE DUE

643919

MARY AND JOHN GRAY LIBRARY
LAMAR UNIVERSITY
BEAUMONT, TEXAS

Eighteenth-Century Florida
The Impact of
the American Revolution

Eighteenth-Century Florida
The Impact of the American Revolution

Bicentennial Symposium, 5th, Pensacola, Fla., 1976.

F
314
B55
1976

Edited by
SAMUEL PROCTOR

643919

LAMAR UNIVERSITY LIBRARY

A University of Florida Book
University Presses of Florida
Gainesville / 1978

Papers read at the Fifth Annual Bicentennial Symposium sponsored by the American Revolution Bicentennial Commission of Florida, held at the University of West Florida, March 18–20, 1976

Library of Congress Cataloging in Publication Data

Bicentennial Symposium, 5th, Pensacola, Fla., 1976.
    Eighteenth-century Florida.

    "A University of Florida book."
    Papers presented at the fifth annual Bicentennial Symposium held March 18–20 and sponsored by the American Revolution Bicentennial Commission of Florida in cooperation with the University of West Florida.
    Includes bibliographical references.
    1. Florida—History—Revolution, 1775–1783—Congresses. 2. Florida—History—English colony, 1763–1784—Congresses. I. Proctor, Samuel. II. American Revolution Bicentennial Commission of Florida. III. University of West Florida. IV. Title.
F314.B55 1976   975.9'02   78–1870
ISBN 0–8130–0589–2

The University Presses of Florida is the scholarly publishing agency for the State University System of Florida.

COPYRIGHT © 1978 BY THE BOARD OF REGENTS
OF THE STATE OF FLORIDA

TYPOGRAPHY BY STORTER PRINTING COMPANY, INCORPORATED
GAINESVILLE, FLORIDA

PRINTED BY ROSE PRINTING COMPANY, INCORPORATED
TALLAHASSEE, FLORIDA

Introduction

UNLIKE the rebelling colonies north of the St. Marys River, the Floridas in 1783 had neither won their independence nor had the territory become part of the American Union. Yet the people who lived in Florida were affected by the peace treaties which ended the Revolution. The most immediate impact, of course, was the return of sovereignty from Britain to Spain. Spain's royal banners flew once more over the vast territory which her conquistadores had discovered in 1513 and which she had held for more than 250 years. Havana, "the Pearl of the Caribbean," had been captured during the Seven Years War, and to redeem that great city, Spain had relinquished with some reluctance her Florida colonies in 1763. Now Spain was returning to that territory which stretched from the Atlantic to the Mississippi and south from the St. Marys to the Keys. Moreover, Spain was determined to hold onto Florida by building up the population, stimulating the economy, and strengthening the defenses; thus the territory could be defended against its old enemy, England, and a new threat, the United States of America.

Except for Gálvez' attack on Pensacola in 1781 and scattered incidents in the Jacksonville–Amelia Island area, the Floridas had not become a theater of military operations during the Revolution. There had been repeated threats of invasion from Georgia and the Carolinas, but none had materialized. A few ship captures and several minor skirmishes were the only military incidents of the war in East Florida. There was no destruction—no real wounds of war—for Florida to recover from after the Revolution. The loyalists who had moved in during the Revolutionary period departed for other destinations when they received word that there would be a change of flags. As refugees, the loyalists had come from Georgia, the Carolinas, and the backcountry. They did not tarry; for the vast majority of them Florida was only a way station. Many returned to their former homes and became loyal Americans; others settled on the Mississippi frontier. Hundreds shipped out of Pensacola and St. Augustine for the Bahamas, Nova Scotia, or England to rebuild their lives and fortunes.

With their departure, Florida became for a brief time almost an empty wilderness. It was history repeating itself, for when the British arrived in 1763, they found that the Spaniards had also departed. Not every Tory, of course, left Florida after 1783; some stayed on believing, or perhaps only hoping, that the United States would not endure and that England would reestablish her sovereignty. And so there remained a Minorcan colony in St. Augustine, English families living along the St. Johns River, and a few French on the Gulf coast in and around Mobile. But the real impact of the American Revolution on Florida was the presence of the United States of America, that newly created country that lay to the north, whose citizens were already dreaming of the day when the American flag would fly over all of North America. Whatever the belief, or hope, on the part of Englishmen living in Florida that America's future was precarious and that its political survival was questionable, Americans were completely optimistic about the future. What better place to expand than south into deserted Florida?

Spain realized that she could not supply what she hoped would be an expanding population with needed manufactures, and she turned to the officials of the Panton, Leslie Company, the English trading firm which had extensive operations in East and West Florida. It had warehouses in St. Augustine and Pensacola, several stores throughout the area, and cordial relations with the Indians in the lower Mississippi Valley.

Aggressive Americans were an ever present problem for Spanish Florida in the years after the American Revolution. Searching always for more land, they poured south, clearing the forests, establishing farms, and planning for the day when the Florida territory would become a part of the United States. By the end of the Revolutionary period a polyglot population had settled in Florida—English, Spanish, French—a vast variety of ethnic, social, and religious groups which lived on and worked the land. In many ways the Floridas were a microcosm of a whole continent. Florida was still unsettled and undeveloped by the close of the eighteenth century, although there had been some economic growth during the British period. Timber had been cut, indigo, cotton, and citrus cultivated, and naval stores and barrel staves exported. The potential for vast social and economic growth in Florida was obvious on every hand.

All of these topics are vital to an understanding of Florida's role during the Revolution and of the impact which it had on the area. The scholars who gathered for the Fifth Florida Bicentennial Symposium in Pensacola, March 18–20, 1976, discussed these and other related subjects. The Bicentennial Symposium was sponsored by the American Revolution Bicentennial Commission of Florida in cooperation with the University of West Florida. There were four previous conferences, beginning with the first held at the University of Florida in 1972. The theme that year was "Eighteenth-Century Florida and Its Borderlands." The following year, 1973, Florida International University helped organize a second symposium in Miami, at which time "Eighteenth-Century Florida and the Caribbean" was the topic for discussion. "Eighteenth-Century Florida: Life on the Frontier" was selected as the theme for the Third Annual Florida Bicentennial Symposium held in Orlando, March 1974, in cooperation with Florida Technological University. The following year, 1975, the fourth symposium, "Eighteenth-Century Florida and the Revolutionary South," was held in Tallahassee in cooperation with Florida State University. Scholarly papers presented at these four conferences have already been published by the University Presses of Florida.

The participants in all of these symposia have included many of the outstanding scholars in American, southern, and Florida colonial history. Their books and monographs and the scholarly articles which they have published in journals both here and abroad have broadened our knowledge and understanding of American history and have helped to shape our thinking and attitudes about Florida's past. The scholars who participated in the fifth symposium examined critically the roles and contributions made by important segments of Florida society during the eighteenth century with special emphasis on the period of the American Revolution.

When the Florida Legislature established the state Bicentennial

viii / Eighteenth-Century Florida and the Revolution

Commission in 1970, it set forth a mandate: plan for Florida's participation in the celebration of our nation's two-hundredth birthday. To recall Florida's heritage, which reaches back more than half a millennium, and to place it in its proper historical perspective became a fundamental goal of the commission. The Committee on Research and Publications developed a comprehensive program of activity which included publication of twenty-five facsimiles of rare, out-of-print books on Florida history, of two volumes devoted to the role of Florida during the Revolutionary period, and of a guidebook to the historic sites that had been placed on the Florida Bicentennial Trail. A series of grants was established to encourage research for and the publication of county and local histories. Almost a score of these works have been published, and several more are in preparation. The commission was a twenty-seven-member body representing the legislature and various state agencies. Ten persons were appointed by the governor, and he served as honorary chairman. Florida's lieutenant governor was the chairman. The commission's executive offices were in Tallahassee.

President James A. Robinson of the University of West Florida welcomed the participants to the Fifth Annual Bicentennial Symposium. Lieutenant Governor Jim Williams, representing the Florida Bicentennial Commission, also extended his greetings to the assemblage. William S. Coker, professor of history, University of West Florida, was chairman of the first session, "The British Floridas." The session "Heritage of Change" was chaired by Professor Jane Dysart of the University of West Florida. Professor James R. McGovern and Professor George F. Pearce served as cochairmen for the session "Florida's People: How They Lived."

The symposium was funded by a special grant from the Bicentennial Commission, and its executive director, Dr. William R. Adams, and his staff were particularly helpful in making arrangements. James Moody, director of the Historic Pensacola Preservation Board, and the local arrangements committee held a reception in the West Florida Museum of History in the historic district of Pensacola for the participants on Thursday evening. Dr. Grier M. Williams directed the West Florida Grand Orchestra in a special concert, "An Evening at Chautauqua," after a dinner on the campus of the University of West Florida Friday evening. Dr. James McGovern was chairman of local arrangements. William Clauss, Jed Mongeon, and the staff of the Division of Continuing Education, University of West Florida, coordinated the arrangements for the meeting.

Dr. Samuel Proctor, Distinguished Service Professor of History and Social Sciences and Julien C. Yonge Professor of Florida History, University of Florida, was chairman of the conference in Pensacola. He served also as chairman of the earlier symposia. The Fifth Annual Bicentennial Symposium was dedicated to the memory of Pat Dodson of Pensacola, former chairman of the American Revolution Bicentennial Commission of Florida.

Symposium Participants

KENNETH COLEMAN, a native of Georgia and a graduate of the University of Georgia, is a longtime member of the history faculty of that institution. He holds his doctorate from the University of Wisconsin. Dr. Coleman is a specialist in Georgia and early American history and has written many articles which have appeared in scholarly journals on these subjects. He is the author of six books, including *Georgia History in Outline, The American Revolution in Georgia, Georgia Journeys, Confederate Athens, Athens, 1861–1865,* and his most recent one, *Colonial Georgia, a History.* He is the editor and one of the contributors to the recently published *History of Georgia.*

THEODORE G. CORBETT is a graduate of Earlham College and of the University of California at Los Angeles and has studied at the University of Madrid and the University of Perugia in Italy. He has been a member of the teaching faculties at the University of Southern California, Wisconsin State University, and Florida State University, and he taught in Florida State University's overseas program in Florence, Italy. Professor Corbett's articles have appeared in the *Journal of the History of Ideas, The Hispanic-American Historical Review,* and the *Florida Historical Quarterly.* He is the author of *The Corporate Spirit in the Reform of Early Modern Spain.* Professor Corbett has worked extensively in the early parish records of Florida to determine migration, population structure, and family life in St. Augustine and East Florida during the First and Second Spanish periods. He has received a grant from the Newberry Library, Chicago, to complete this Florida study.

ANNA C. EBERLY is a native of Richmond, Virginia, and attended the Virginia Commonwealth University. She works for the National Park Service as an interpretive specialist in eighteenth-century history and is presently serving as interpretive supervisor at Turkey Run Farm, McLean, Virginia. The St. Augustine Preservation Board and other professional agencies in the United States and in Puerto Rico have utilized her extensive knowledge of fabrics and colonial-period clothing.

MICHAEL V. GANNON, a specialist in Florida religious history, is a graduate of the University of Florida, a professor of religion and history at that institution, and assistant dean of the College of Arts and Sciences. Professor Gannon has had a longtime interest in the early Spanish missions of Florida and has written about them extensively. Two of his books, *Rebel Bishop* and *The Cross and the Sand*, treat the early history of the Roman Catholic Church in Florida. He edited and wrote the introduction to George Fairbanks' *History and Antiquities of the City of St. Augustine, Florida*, one of the volumes in the Bicentennial Floridiana Facsimile Series. His articles have appeared in scholarly and professional journals, and he was the first recipient of the Arthur W. Thompson Memorial Prize in Florida History given by the Florida Historical Society. Dr. Gannon is chairman of the Historic St. Augustine Preservation Board and serves as chairman of the advisory board for the southeastern states to the National Park Service. The government of Spain has bestowed upon him the Knight Cross of the Order of Isabella.

THOMAS G. LEDFORD is a native of Houston, Texas, and holds his graduate degrees from the University of Arizona. He served as associate curator in the exhibit division of Arizona State University before coming to St. Augustine in 1973 as restoration curator. He was involved in the Historic Preservation Board's interpretation of that colonial city, including research of the material culture, archeology, and exhibit planning. His interests include the history of American technology and early American industries, Spanish-Colonial material culture, and military history.

ALBERT MANUCY, a native of St. Augustine, received his degrees from the University of Florida and has served as historian, restorationist, interpretive planner, and curator with the National Park Service, United States Department of the Interior. Since 1971 he has been a free-lance writer, illustrator, and historical consultant, working for the St. Augustine Restoration Foundation, the National Geographic Society, and other organizations. He was a Fulbright Research Scholar in Spain and has received awards from the United States Department of the Interior, the Amigos los Castillos of Spain, and Rollins College. Mr. Manucy is a past president of the Florida Historical Society and has contributed many articles to scholarly and professional journals. His books and monographs include *Artillery Through the Ages, Colonial Floors at Castillo de San Marcos, The Fort at Frederica, The Houses of St. Augustine, Florida's Menéndez,* and *The Forts of Old San Juan.*

GEORGE C. ROGERS, JR., was born in Charleston, South Carolina, and is a graduate of the College of Charleston and the University of Chicago. He was selected as a Rotary International Foundation Fellow in 1949–50 and studied at the Univesrity of Edinburgh, Scotland. Before his appointment to the faculty of history at the University of South Carolina in 1958, Dr. Rogers taught American history at the University of Pennsylvania, Hunter College, and Emory University. He is presently Yates Snowden Professor of History at the University of South Carolina. In addition to many scholarly articles, Dr. Rogers is the author of *Evolution of a Federalist, Charleston in the Age of the Pinckneys,* and *The History of Georgetown County, South Carolina.* He is the editor of the *South Carolina Historical Magazine* and served as a member of both the South Carolina Tricentennial Commission and the advisory committee for the Library of Congress American Revolution Bicentennial program. He is also editor of *The Papers of Henry Laurens.*

ROBERT A. RUTLAND, a native of Okmulgee, Oklahoma, was educated at the University of Oklahoma, Cornell University, and Vanderbilt University. After working as a reporter for the United Press in Oklahoma City, he became research associate for the State Historical Society of Iowa. He taught journalism at the University of California, Los Angeles, from 1954 to 1969, and held a one-year appointment as Fulbright professor at the University of Innsbruck, Austria. He was coordinator of Bicentennial programs (1969-71) at the Library of Congress, and it was during this period that he edited three volumes of *The Papers of George Mason.* Since 1971 Professor Rutland has been professor of history at the University of Virginia and editor of *The James Madison Papers.* He is the author and editor of a number of books, including *The Birth of the Bill of Rights, George Mason, Reluctant Statesman, The Ordeal of the Constitution,* and *The Newsmongers.* His most recent publication is *Madison's Alternatives: The Jeffersonian Republicans and the Coming of War, 1805-1812.*

J. BARTON STARR, a native Floridian, born in Pensacola, received his degrees from Samford University and Florida State University. He is a member of the history faculty of Troy State University at Fort Rucker, Alabama. His articles have appeared in the *Florida Historical Quarterly,* the *Alabama Review,* and other professional journals, and his book, *Tories, Dons, and Rebels: The American Revolution in British West Florida, 1775-1783,* has been published by the University Presses of Florida. He is also coauthor of *Alabama in the Nation* and has edited John Pope's *Tour through the Southern and Western Territories* in the Bicentennial Floridiana Facsimile Series.

J. LEITCH WRIGHT, JR., a graduate of the University of Virginia, is professor of history at Florida State University. Prior to coming to Florida he taught at the Virginia Military Institute and Randolph-Macon College. Professor Wright is a specialist in eighteenth- and nineteenth-century southern and Florida history, and his articles on these subjects have appeared in many scholarly journals. He is the author of the monograph, *British St. Augustine,* and his books include: *William Augustus Bowles: Director General of the Creek*

Nation, Anglo-Spanish Rivalry in North America, Britain and the American Frontier, 1783–1815, and *Florida in the American Revolution.* The latter volume was commissioned by the American Revolution Bicentennial Commission of Florida. Professor Wright is a member of the Board of Directors of the Florida Historical Society and serves on the editorial board of the *Florida Historical Quarterly.*

Contents

British East Florida: Loyalist Bastion / J. Leitch Wright / 1

"Left as a Gewgaw": The Impact of the American Revolution on British West Florida / J. Barton Starr / 14

Commentary / George C. Rogers, Jr. / 28

The Southern Contribution: A Balance Sheet on the War for Independence / Robert A. Rutland / 38

The Problem of the Household in the Second Spanish Period / Theodore G. Corbett / 49

Mitres and Flags: Colonial Religion in the British and Second Spanish Periods / Michael V. Gannon / 76

Commentary / Kenneth Coleman / 93

Changing Traditions in St. Augustine Architecture / Albert Manucy / 99

British Material Culture in St. Augustine: The Artifact as Social Commentary / Thomas G. Ledford / 133

What Our Southern Frontier Women Wore / Anna C. Eberly / 143

British East Florida: Loyalist Bastion

J. Leitch Wright

PRECEDING the outbreak of hostilities in 1775 and throughout the entire American Revolution the royal province of East Florida was conspicuous for its loyalty to the Crown. From the battles of Lexington and Concord until the final evacuation in 1784, the Union Jack resolutely waved over St. Augustine for nine years. This was a longer period than for any other comparable mainland colony. East Florida's conduct contrasted with that of the thirteen colonies to the north who overthrew British rule. Yet by taking a larger view it is apparent that East Florida's course was not so exceptional. In addition to the thirteen which rebelled, Britain had other American colonies which remained loyal, including West Florida, Quebec, Nova Scotia, Newfoundland, Jamaica, Barbados, and other West Indian islands. The total numbered some thirty. All of them were affected by Parliament's revenue measures, the navigation acts, and mercantilistic restrictions imposed by the Mother Country, and all complained before 1775 about aspects of imperial rule.

During 1775-76 Britain's colonies in the Western Hemisphere had to decide whether the Mother Country's regulations were so onerous that independence was the only recourse. With great reluctance in some cases, thirteen decided on separation, while the other seventeen refused to draw their swords against the Crown, remaining in the empire despite its imperfections. East Florida followed this latter course as did most of Britain's New World colonies, and in this sense, East Florida was in the mainstream and her thirteen neighbors were out of step. It should be kept in mind, how-

2 / Eighteenth-Century Florida and the Revolution

ever, that with few exceptions it was Britain's most populous colonies which revolted and the most thinly settled ones, such as East Florida, which did not.

A number of general reasons help explain East Florida's loyalty and that of many other British colonies in America. First to be considered is imperial taxation. East Floridians grumbled about the Stamp Act. After 1763, the new colony was caught up in the frenetic land speculation raging throughout America, and vexatious stamps had to be placed on legal documents, increasing the costs of land acquisition. Stamps also had to be placed on newspapers, but this was not a great burden since until 1783 no paper was printed in the province. East Floridians like other Americans were not enthusiastic about paying Stamp Act taxes, the Townshend Duty Act imposts, and duties on tea. The important point to keep in mind, however, is that British East Florida, like Spanish Florida beforehand, was subsidized by the Mother Country.[1]

East Floridians recognized that the amount of money spent in the province by the Crown greatly exceeded the taxes collected. The Mother Country paid the salaries of royal officials, built barracks, a powder magazine, a hospital, and provincial fortifications and spent large sums to support a garrison of regulars numbering between two hundred and six hundred and fifty men before 1775. Approximately one-twentieth of the British army in America was stationed in East Florida,[2] while most of the thirteen colonies had no redcoats, certainly not in their capitals. If East Floridians proclaimed their independence they would have to tax themselves for the first time to pay for provincial defense and civil government. These taxes would have fallen primarily on an influential white elite who were well aware of this fact. Imperial revenue measures which helped sever the bonds of empire in the thirteen colonies served to fix East Florida firmly in the Old Empire.

Continued necessity for British protection was another influence helping keep East Florida loyal. The province confronted a number of potential dangers: large Indian and Negro populations, each of which outnumbered whites, an exposed coastline vulnerable to insult from Spanish and French warships, and a small—and if one

---

1. Wilfred B. Kerr, "The Stamp Act in the Floridas, 1765–1766," *Journal of American History* 21 (1935):463–70.
2. Charles L. Mowat, "St. Francis Barracks, St. Augustine: A Link with the British Regime," *Florida Historical Quarterly* 21 (1943):267–68.

British East Florida / 3

included Catholic Minorcans[3]—perhaps unreliable provincial militia. Britain's other colonies which remained loyal in 1775 still felt the need of the Mother Country's protection. Perhaps 90 percent of the inhabitants of the province of Quebec were French speaking, and British rulers realized they were in a minority and that France might try to revenge Montcalm's loss on the Plains of Abraham.[4] Nova Scotia, though part of the American mainland, in fact was isolated and appreciated the need of British protection. West Floridians merely had to look across their river boundaries to see enemy Spanish soldiers, while the island of Jamaica depended on the Royal Navy for its survival. Virginia, Massachusetts, and the colonies which revolted felt that enemy threats were insignificant after 1763. Had not France departed from Canada and Louisiana, and Spain given up Florida, and could not the thirteen colonies rely on a numerous militia to quell local disturbances? The thirteen colonies had not been taxed for imperial defense before 1763 and saw even less need for assuming this burden after the Seven Years War, now that France and Spain were gone. This reasoning made sense in Williamsburg and Boston but not in St. Augustine.

The very presence of the British army—and to an extent the Royal Navy—in East Florida had much to do with the province's loyalty. It was the army, not civilians, who took over St. Augustine from the Spaniards, and for twenty-one years, until the final evacuation, redcoats were evident throughout the province. They garrisoned redoubtable Fort St. Marks and transformed the four-story coquina Franciscan monastery on the capital's southern edge into a barracks. If soldiers were not quartered in the fort or in the St. Francis Barracks, they moved into deserted houses in town, which had belonged to the Spaniards who had departed almost without exception. With bright red coats, freshly tarred gaiters, and long bayonets hanging from their belts, troops, marching at quickstep back and forth between the barracks and fort through St. Augustine's narrow streets, deterred any incipient rebel.[5]

---

3. Governor Tonyn continually fretted that Catholic Minorcans would collaborate with their coreligionists in Spain and France or possibly with American Whigs. Minorcans did correspond with Spaniards in Cuba, though on the whole Minorcans did not support Britain's enemies.
4. William J. Eccles, *France in America* (New York, 1972), pp. 228–38.
5. The British occupation of St. Augustine and the establishment of British rule may be followed in my *British St. Augustine* (St. Augustine, 1975), pp. 1ff.

4 / Eighteenth-Century Florida and the Revolution

Even if a potential Sam Adams or Patrick Henry had appeared in East Florida's capital, there was no convenient sanctuary within the province for him to retreat to and be protected by supporters. Other than New Smyrna seventy miles below St. Augustine, no significant body of whites lived in the province. For a combination of reasons New Smyrna was not a safe haven for potential rebels. Had a Sam Adams or a Patrick Henry been inclined to speak out in St. Augustine he probably would have had to retire to an adjoining colony. East Florida in fact had no incendiaries of this type. Royal Governor Patrick Tonyn accused Andrew Turnbull, New Smyrna's proprietor, and Chief Justice William Drayton of secretly sympathizing with those Americans proclaiming independence, and there may have been truth in these charges. Tonyn badgered Turnbull and Drayton, forced both of them out of the province during the Revolution, and before the war was over, they had taken up permanent residence in South Carolina.[6]

The absence of a popular assembly was another reason no fiery radicals emerged in East Florida before 1775. Both Henry and Adams had used the elected assembly effectively as a forum in their respective provinces. The Royal Proclamation of 1763 stipulated that the government of East Florida would be patterned after that of typical royal colonies such as Virginia and Massachusetts.[7] Provision was made for an appointed governor and council and a representative lower house. As it turned out East Florida's first assembly did not meet until March, 1781, and its sessions continued for over two years until the end of 1783.[8] Governor Tonyn, who confronted many problems in 1775, was relieved that a hostile assembly was not one of them.

So far in explaining in a general way why East Floridians did not revolt in 1775 there has been the tendency to lump all the province's population together. This is misleading because East Florida's populace was heterogeneous. A casual visitor in 1775 might have

6. Charles L. Mowat, *East Florida as a British Province, 1763-1784* (1943, facsimile reprint, ed. Rembert W. Patrick, Gainesville, Fla., 1964), pp. 83-106.

7. The proclamation is published in Adam Shortt and Arthur G. Doughty, eds., *Documents Relating to the Constitutional History of Canada, 1759-1791* (Ottawa, 1918) 1:163-68.

8. Debates and proceedings of the East Florida assembly are in Great Britain, Public Record Office (hereafter cited as P.R.O.), CO5/572 and 624.

heard snatches of English, French, Spanish, Catalan, Greek, Italian, Sicilian, German, Muskogee, Hitchiti, Cherokee, Mende, Hausa, Fulani, a pidgin such as Gullah, and a Scottish burr. Sometimes ethnic groups remained doggedly loyal for different reasons.

In East Florida, as in Georgia and South Carolina, whites were in the minority. Among the whites the Scots were prominent: the province's first governor, James Grant; the men of the Royal Scots regiment who occupied St. Augustine in 1763 and took their discharges in the capital; Anglican priest the Reverend John Forbes, a graduate of King's College, Aberdeen; merchant-planter Richard Oswald, friend of Benjamin Franklin and Henry Laurens and master of Mount Oswald on the Tomoka River; James Spalding, who maintained Indian trading posts on the St. Johns River; these, with many others, both civilians and in the military, testified to the omnipresence of the Scottish influence. It is not that Scots played such an important role in East Florida that is controversial, but instead why almost all of them in East Florida and throughout America remained so fiercely loyal to the Mother Country. The occasional Scottish John Paul Jones was the exception. Highlander and Lowlander alike served George III faithfully in America. This seems perplexing, for Highlanders had been ruthlessly suppressed by royal forces after their defeat at Culloden in 1745, and they had seen their clan system and tartans proscribed. Yet three decades later there were no more active champions of royal government in America than Highlanders. James Cameron of the Royal Scots, mustered out in St. Augustine after the 1763 peace, took up arms again during the Revolution and died fighting for the Crown in Georgia.[9]

One explanation of Highlander loyalty is that the 1745 hostilities reflected almost as much inter-clan rivalry as a conflict with the British king.[10] Economic motives probably better account for the devotion of both Highlanders and Lowlanders to the preservation of the empire. Scotland agreed to the 1707 union with England primarily for economic reasons. As a result the British empire in America was thrown open to ambitious Scotsmen, and during the eighteenth century they eagerly took advantage of their opportunity.

9. Memorial of Ann Cameron, Jan. 23, 1787, P.R.O. Audit Office (hereafter cited as A.O.), 12/3.
10. George S. Pryde, *Scotland from 1603 to the Present Day* (Edinburgh, 1962), pp. 57–66.

6 / Eighteenth-Century Florida and the Revolution

When Britain acquired East Florida, Scottish soldiers, civil servants, merchants, artisans, and land speculators were among the first on the scene. Absentee planter-merchant Richard Oswald not only acquired Mount Oswald in East Florida but also had holdings in Georgia, the West Indies, England, and Africa.[11] In large measure his affluence depended on the thriving commercial capitalism and security guaranteed by the empire. There is every reason to assume that the fortunes of less wealthy Scots in East Florida were similarly identified with the preservation of the empire. There is another possible explanation of Scottish loyalty. Throughout British America they were frequently disliked and distrusted by non-Gaelic neighbors, and Scots may have felt that their minority interests would be best served by a powerful government in London.[12]

Minorcans comprised another significant group of whites in East Florida. In the late 1760s, Andrew Turnbull had engaged impoverished peasants from Minorca, along with others from Greece, Italy, and Sicily, to emigrate to New Smyrna. Revolts, beatings, sickness, and a high death toll followed, and Turnbull's experiment fared poorly. Minorcans blamed Turnbull for much of their suffering. This rather than imperial taxation was their greatest concern in 1775. Surviving Minorcans, numbering some four hundred in 1777, deserted New Smyrna en masse, marched to St. Augustine, and threw themselves on the mercy of Governor Tonyn. Minorcans had fled from Turnbull, who was accused of secretly being a Whig, into the arms of their savior, Governor Tonyn, who was very much a Tory.[13]

East Florida Indians fought valiantly in behalf of George III. Tribes which had lived in Florida at the time of sixteenth-century white contact for the most part had disappeared. Newcomers, typically Hitchiti-speaking Lower Creeks, had moved southward in the eighteenth century to fill the vacuum. At some point, apparently early in the British period, they were called Seminoles.[14] Concentrated in Alachua, Apalache, and about the forks of the Apalachicola

11. Memorial of Mary Oswald, Nov. 11, 1786, P.R.O., A.O. 12/3.
12. William H. Nelson, *The American Tory* (Oxford, 1961), p. 89.
13. Several books have been written about the Turnbull colony at New Smyrna; the most recent is Jane Quinn, *Minorcans in Florida: Their History and Heritage* (St. Augustine, 1975). Miss Quinn erroneously equates the sufferings of the New Smyrna bondsmen with those grievances about which Patrick Henry and Sam Adams were complaining.
14. The best account of the origin of the Florida Seminoles is Charles H. Fairbanks, *Ethnohistorical Report on the Florida Indians* (New York, 1974).

River, Seminoles and Lower Creeks fought side by side with redcoats. Thomas Brown, wealthy refugee from the Georgia–South Carolina backcountry, had been tarred and feathered at the beginning of the Revolution. Arriving in East Florida, he became a colonel in the provincial forces, and in 1779, the Crown appointed him Indian superintendent. More often than not it was Brown who was at the head of the Indians whenever Georgians invaded East Florida, and it was Superintendent Brown who later led warriors northward across the St. Marys River into Georgia and South Carolina.[15]

The conduct of East Florida Indians during the Revolution was similar to that of natives from the Gulf of Mexico to Canada. It did not make much difference to them whether George III, Louis XVI of France, Charles III of Spain, or George Washington was their white father. The overriding consideration was which country through trade and presents could furnish the Indians manufactured goods and at the same time not overrun their lands. After 1775, it appeared that Britain was best suited for this role. Through an unplanned series of developments Britain had assumed France's former position on the North American mainland. Rebellious Whigs in the thirteen colonies threatened Indian lands, while Britain, the leading industrial nation, backed by a powerful navy, controlled St. Augustine and later Savannah in the South and Detroit and Montreal in the North. British subjects were best able to furnish the required manufactures. East Florida Seminoles, dressed in scarlet coats, armed with steel knives and hatchets, wearing silver armbands and gorgets, and equipped with new muskets and rifles, all recently made in England, lifted Whig scalps throughout the war.[16]

Blacks comprised the largest ethnic group in East Florida and outnumbered whites roughly two to one. Some were free; others as either slaves or freemen lived among the Indians, while a majority were slaves who worked in rice, indigo, and sugar fields or produced naval stores on St. Johns and St. Marys river plantations. Blacks

---

15. Brown's career can be followed in excellent articles by Gary D. Olson, "Loyalists and the American Revolution: Thomas Brown and the South Carolina Backcountry, 1775–1776," *South Carolina Historical Magazine* 68 (1967):201–19, 69 (1968):44–56; and "Thomas Brown, Loyalist Partisan, and the Revolutionary War in Georgia, 1777–1782," *Georgia Historical Quarterly* 54 (1970):1–19, 183–208.

16. My *Britain and the American Frontier, 1783–1815* (Athens, Ga., 1975) considers the implications of Britain's assuming the previous French position in North America.

numbered just over two thousand in 1775, and by 1783, their numbers had swelled to approximately ten thousand.[17] Because of the dearth of sources—far more scarce than for neighboring Georgia and South Carolina—it is risky to speculate about the response of East Florida blacks to the Revolution. Based on such evidence as is available one might guess that they were little affected by rebel arguments concerning natural rights and imperial taxation. In most respects it made little difference whether a slave's master was Whig or Tory.

Throughout the South slaves were numerous, and in the lower South, including East Florida, they were in a majority. The military potential of blacks was not lost on hard-pressed royal officials. Governor Dunmore in Virginia, Lord Cornwallis in the Carolinas, Governor Tonyn in East Florida all at the outset expected blacks to support the royal cause in a variety of ways. They might serve as impressed laborers, be organized into military units as pioneers, or be given muskets and employed as ordinary soldiers. At the beginning of the Revolution royal authorities from Virginia to Georgia promised slaves who ran away from their Whig masters sanctuary and freedom within British lines.[18] Because there were no Whig plantations in East Florida and his authority was not threatened, Governor Tonyn did not have to issue such a proclamation. It is reasonable to assume, however, that East Florida Negroes who served with distinction in military units expected to win their freedom. Most of East Florida's new black population came from Georgia and South Carolina where British commanders for years had promised freedom to fugitive slaves. During the war both southern Whigs and Tories talked a good deal about natural rights and the evils of slavery; for the most part, however, it was Tories who at times backed up their oratory with deeds. A tradition evolved that, at least to a degree, black freedom was linked to the success of the

17. Mowat, *East Florida*, p. 137; J. Leitch Wright, Jr., *Florida in the American Revolution* (Gainesville, Fla., 1975), p. 13. Population figures are estimates and do not include blacks living among the Indians.

18. Benjamin Quarles, *The Negro in the American Revolution* (Chapel Hill, 1961), pp. 19–32; James Wright, John Graham, Anthony Stokes, et al. to Lord Germain, in Wright to Germain, 6 Jan. 1779, *Collections of the Georgia Historical Society* (Savannah, 1873), 3:250; memoranda for the Commandant of Charleston and for Lord Cornwallis, Charleston, 3 June 1780, Sir Guy Carleton Papers, 2800, London, microfilm, Florida State University Library.

royal cause. This helps explain why East Florida Negroes either remained passive or actively fought for George III.[19]

We leave the blacks and the Indians to look more closely at the white elite. Whether they were Scots, Englishmen, or immigrants from other British colonies in America, a high percentage of these whites were royal officials, including the governor, lieutenant governor, councilmen, surveyor, priest, schoolmaster, harbor pilot, clerk of the council, messenger of the council, sheriff, naval officer, jailer, constables, receiver general of the quit rents, clerk of the public accounts, keeper of the Indian presents, deputy postmaster, judge and court officials, customs officers, provost marshal, coroner, etc. With few exceptions their salaries were paid by a parliamentary subsidy.[20] Throughout America crown officials tended to remain loyal, and East Florida was no exception. The difference was that in East Florida royal officials did not comprise an insignificant white minority.

In discussing East Florida's population, so far only males, explicitly or by inference, have been considered. British East Florida was a raw, new colony and, as was typical of almost anywhere on the American frontier, males outnumbered females two or three to one. For lack of any contrary evidence it must be assumed that the political views of the wives of planters, artisans, soldiers, merchants, and agricultural laborers were the same as their husbands'. Few single white females appeared in British East Florida, and widows with any spark or fortune remaining soon remarried.[21]

East Florida's population, excluding Indians and the garrison, grew from approximately four thousand in 1775 to over seventeen thousand in 1783.[22] Many of the newcomers had been tarred and feathered or otherwise abused, had had their property confiscated, and had been forced to flee precipitately. These uncompromising loyalists proved the most zealous champions of George III's govern-

---

19. See James W. St. G. Walker's perceptive article, "Blacks as American Loyalists: The Slaves' War for Independence," *Historical Reflections* 2 (1975): 51–67.

20. John Pownall to Peter Chester, Whitehall, 3 May 1775, Colonial Office Records (hereafter cited as C.O.), 5/619.

21. Mary Peavett is perhaps St. Augustine's best-known widow. She married three husbands in succession, the last of whom was half her age. St. Augustine Historical Society, *The Oldest House* (St. Augustine, 1963), p. 5.

22. Mowat, *East Florida*, p. 137.

ment. Most of them believed in representative government and no taxation without representation. They merely felt that their interests would be best served by remaining in the empire. Their increasing presence in East Florida made that province even more loyal after 1775 than it had been previously. Refugees eagerly enlisted in provincial units raised in East Florida. Whether combating Americans who tried to liberate St. Augustine early in the Revolution or later fighting in Georgia and South Carolina, these displaced Tories participated in some of the most savage fighting of the war.

After Lexington and Concord the size of the regular army stationed in East Florida increased, though at first the withdrawal of troops from the province to others more threatened had reduced the number of effective soldiers to barely thirty-five able-bodied men.[23] But in 1776, reinforcements arrived, and for the balance of the war, between just under five hundred and over three thousand enlisted men speaking assorted English dialects, German, and French were stationed in the province.[24] Usually the total was closer to the lower figure. Soldiers were not necessarily the flower of European society, and harsh penalities of up to five hundred lashes and execution by firing squads seemed necessary to preserve discipline. Occasionally disputes between the St. Augustine garrison and civilians got out of hand. Soldiers patronized conveniently located taverns. If for some reason they were not satisfied with the service, off-duty redcoats might pull down the building, timber by timber. Soldiers sometimes assumed that the women who fetched their rum also practiced an older profession. A melee ensued whenever a redcoat erred.[25] There was probably some truth to reports reaching the Continental Congress that enlisted men in East Florida's garrison were unhappy and might desert.[26]

Occasional civilian-military altercations and possibly a raid on

23. John Stuart to Major Small, St. Augustine, 2 Oct. 1775, Peter Force, ed., *American Archives: Consisting of a Collection of Authentick Records, State Papers, Debates, and Letters and Other Notices of Public Affairs . . . Fourth Series* (Washington, 1837–53), 4:318.
24. Sir Henry Clinton to Lord George Germain, 8 Oct. 1778, Sir Henry Clinton Papers, William L. Clements Library, Ann Arbor, Michigan; state of the army under the command of Clinton, New York, 15 Feb. 1781, ibid.
25. Patrick Tonyn to Germain, St. Augustine, 26 Nov. 1781, C.O. 5/560.
26. Memorial and particulars relative to Ft. St. Augustine with a plan of attack, by Marquis de Bretigny, 26 Aug. 1778, U.S. Continental Congress, papers of the Continental Congress, 1774–89, National Archives and Record Service, microfilm, Florida State University Library.

British East Florida / 11

the coast by an enemy privateer marked the only disturbances in East Florida after 1778. The growing population seemed secure, wartime demands stimulated the economy, and the first provincial representative assembly was elected and met in 1781. Yet not many months transpired after delegates commenced deliberations in the state house before news arrived of Cornwallis' disaster at Yorktown. During the 1782-83 peace negotiations East Florida's fate was a lively topic. Throughout the Revolution East Floridians had suffered and fought in George III's behalf, and they had resolutely kept the province in the empire. They were stunned, therefore, when they learned in 1783 that the colony was to be handed over to Spain.

Though the peace treaty allowed British subjects to keep their property and remain in the province, a majority elected to move elsewhere. They relocated in Nova Scotia, the Mother Country, the West Indies, and especially the neighboring Bahama Islands; some moved to the Mississippi Valley or returned to their homes in the United States. The harbor at St. Augustine and the mouth of the St. Marys River were busier than ever after 1783 evacuating white loyalists along with blacks and a few Indians. The formal transfer of power occurred in St. Augustine on July 12, 1784, and Governor Tonyn and the remainder of the exiles did not leave the St. Marys River until the end of 1785.[27]

In many respects this British evacuation duplicated the Spanish one in 1763. The main difference was that, whereas, with minor exceptions, all Spaniards had left Florida, a considerable number of British loyalists remained. In a variety of ways they would help shape Florida's development both during the Second Spanish Period and later, when the Americans took over. Among those who stayed, Minorcans were the most conspicuous, cohesive group. Spain's insistence on Catholic orthodoxy posed no problem for them. In the decades after the Revolution some Minorcans rose from an oppressed peasantry and achieved a measure of prosperity and influence. The Benét family was an example, and in 1845 the first cadet appointed to West Point from the new state of Florida was Stephen Vincent Benét, grandfather of the twentieth-century poet.[28] Joseph M. Hernandez, the military officer who captured Osceola

27. Wilbur H. Siebert, ed., *Loyalists in East Florida, 1774-1785; The Most Important Documents Pertaining Thereto, Edited with an Accompanying Narrative by Wilbur Henry Siebert* (DeLand, Fla., 1929), 1:137-80.
28. Charles A. Fenton, *Stephen Vincent Benét: The Life and Times of an American Man of Letters, 1898-1943* (New Haven, 1958), p. 4.

12 / Eighteenth-Century Florida and the Revolution

in the Second Seminole War, also was of Minorcan background.[29] Swiss-born Francis Philip Fatio, a professional soldier in Britain's garrison during the Revolution, remained after 1785. The Ximenez-Fatio house in St. Augustine is one of the older surviving structures and indicates the important nineteenth-century role played by the Fatio progeny. Former British subjects remained on their property in St. Augustine or on their St. Marys and St. Johns river plantations; others who initially had evacuated the province were enticed back by Spain to help develop East Florida. Zephaniah Kingsley, ebullient master of Kingsley Plantation, falls into this category.[30]

Indians and even blacks remained in East Florida after the Revolution and remained loyal to the British interest largely because British merchants traded with them and encouraged them to hold fast to their lands, culture, and liberty. Typical merchants and "political advisers" who lived among the Indians and blacks were former British loyalists or their descendants and business associates. One merely has to mention Thomas Brown, William Augustus Bowles, George Woodbine, Alexander Arbuthnot, and Robert Ambrister—the latter two executed at St. Marks by Andrew Jackson in 1818—to make the point. From the American Revolution until at least the conclusion of the Second Seminole War, East Florida blacks and Indians continued to fight against the Americans. Seminole Chief Kinache (Kinhega) had marched with Thomas Brown during the Revolution and with Bowles afterwards, accompanied British troops to New Orleans in 1814, and confronted Andrew Jackson and his American successors when they stormed into East Florida. Up until his death (in the 1820s or perhaps later) he regarded British loyalists as his allies and looked to King George as his protector.[31]

British loyalists still dominated Florida's commerce after the Revolution. Before the war William Panton, from his base in Georgia, had traded with East Florida Indians; he fled from Georgia after the outbreak of hostilities, and Governor Tonyn entrusted him with

29. John K. Mahon, *History of the Second Seminole War, 1835–1842* (Gainesville, Fla., 1967), p. 99; Quinn, *Minorcans in Florida*, p. 164.

30. There is no biography of Kingsley, and there is not likely to be a satisfactory one until historians make further researches into East Florida's Second Spanish Period. A starting point is Philip S. May, "Zephaniah Kingsley, Nonconformist (1765–1843)," *Florida Historical Quarterly* 23 (1945):145–59.

31. George Woodbine to Hugh Pigot, Prospect Bluff, 25 May 1814, Cochrane Papers, National Library of Scotland, Edinburgh, 2328; William V. Munnings to Lord Bathurst, Nassau, 30 Nov. 1918, C.O. 23/68.

overseeing East Florida's Indian commerce; after the Revolution Panton's partners remained in East Florida and, with Spain's blessing, enjoyed in effect a monopoly of the Indian trade. John Leslie, a member of Panton, Leslie and Company, stayed in St. Augustine, supervised his agents at warehouses on the St. Johns and St. Marys rivers, and legally or not, traded extensively with the populace of Spanish St. Augustine.[32] William Panton joined the general evacuation from St. Augustine and retired to the Bahamas, though by 1785 he had relocated in Pensacola. As much as anyone he helped make Pensacola the dominant port for the Indian trade of the entire Old Southwest, supplanting Charleston and Savannah. He prospered more than ever at Pensacola and probably was the most affluent inhabitant in Spanish West Florida.[33]

By moving into Pensacola Panton's East Florida firm took over the pre-Revolutionary Indian trade formerly controlled by other British merchants in West Florida. These West Florida merchants had been forced to evacuate Pensacola after the 1781 capitulation to Spain, and Panton and his East Florida associates saw their opportunity and eagerly filled the vacuum. Part of Spanish West Florida's stormy history after the Revolution represented a conflict between Tory newcomers from East Florida, like Panton, and former British West Floridians, such as the merchant and councilman John Miller, who had to abandon Pensacola in 1781.[34] But merely looking at the career of William Panton and John Leslie is enough to illustrate that militant loyalists in diverse ways continued to play a substantial role throughout both East and West Florida long after the passions of the Revolutionary War had subsided.

32. Janice B. Miller, "Juan Nepomuceno de Quesada, Spanish Governor of East Florida 1790–1795" (Ph.D. diss., Florida State University, 1974), p. 197.
33. Randy Nimnicht, "William Panton: His Early Career on the Changing Frontier" (Master's thesis, University of Florida, 1968) gives the best account of Panton's pre-1783 career, and other scholars have dealt with Panton, Leslie and Company after the Revolution. In this latter regard one should be aware of the forthcoming Papers of Panton, Leslie and Company, William S. Coker, University of West Florida, editor and project director.
34. The West Florida planter-merchant John Miller relocated in the Bahama Islands after the Revolution and in time became the senior member of the Bahamian council. In conjunction with exiled Florida merchants, Lord Dunmore (the Bahamian governor), William Augustus Bowles, and others, Miller for years attempted to reestablish his commerce in West Florida.

"Left as a Gewgaw":

The Impact of the American Revolution

on British West Florida

J. BARTON STARR

WHEN West Florida became a British possession at the conclusion of the French and Indian War in 1763, Great Britain found itself the guardian of a sparsely settled, unhealthy, and dilapidated piece of real estate. Twenty years later England returned the province to Spain with larger towns, better fortifications, and a much larger population which was capable of producing royal revenues through various crops; in general, Spain received back a considerably more valuable colony. The intervening twenty years form the history of British West Florida, a history filled with growth, internal discord, the American Revolution, loyalty, and the war with Spain. It is at times a dull and almost lifeless history; at times one of excitement, heroics, and pageantry; and at times a history filled with death, defeat, and pathos.

The story of the American Revolution and the concomitant Anglo-Spanish war in West Florida fills almost half of the brief history of the British possession of the colony. The province was a frontier area, remote from the scene of the Revolution, at peace but in fear of war. In the years preceding the outbreak of hostilities, there was little to indicate that West Floridians were even aware of the problems to the north which would eventually lead to war. With the exception of the Stamp Act—to which there was noisy but fruitless opposition—the causes of unrest in the American colonies which are traditionally considered as leading to the rebellion had little meaning for West Floridians.[1]

1. J. Barton Starr, " 'The Spirit of What Is There Called Liberty': The

Impact of the American Revolution / 15

During the first three years of the rebellion, West Florida was cognizant of the war only through correspondence and occasional rebel excursions to New Orleans for supplies. The request from the First Continental Congress that West Florida endorse their actions was shelved by Governor Peter Chester and never made public. Likewise, the Continental Association, the prohibition on trade to West Florida by the Continental Congress, and the embargo placed on commerce with the rebellious colonies by Lord George Germain, had little effect on the colony.[2]

The earliest result of the American Revolution that had an impact on West Florida was the influx of loyalists from the thirteen colonies in rebellion. As early as May 1774, a West Floridian suggested that if immigration to West Florida were "properly encouraged, [it] would greatly aid in purging and regulating the discontented colonies."[3] Apparently the next mention of the matter was not until July 5, 1775, when the Earl of Dartmouth informed Governor Chester of a ministerial decision concerning the loyalists. Dartmouth instructed Chester to issue a proclamation declaring West Florida to be a haven for loyalists fleeing the colonies in rebellion and promising land grants in the colony for the newcomers.[4] Chester issued the required proclamation on November 11, 1775,[5] and while the refugees were slow in coming at first, by April 1776 the loyalists were flocking to West Florida in large numbers. As a result of this loyalist immigration, the population of West Florida nearly doubled during the American Revolution. The loyalists who sought asylum in West Florida came from almost every colony in revolt as well as East Florida and the West Indies. Over 40 percent of those for

---

Stamp Act in British West Florida," *Alabama Review* (July 1976). See also my "Tories, Dons, and Rebels: The American Revolution in British West Florida, 1775–1783" (Ph.D. diss., Florida State University, 1971), pp. 71–80, recently published in revised form (Gainesville, Fla., 1976).

2. Worthington C. Ford et al., eds., *Journals of the Continental Congress, 1774–1789* (Washington, 1904–37), 1:101–3, 54; Henry Middleton (president of Congress) to the inhabitants of West Florida, 22 Oct. 1774, Colonial Office 5/595 (hereafter cited C.O.); Peter Chester to George Germain, 24 Nov. 1778, ibid.; Germain to the governors of the West Indian Islands, Nova Scotia, East and West Florida, 1 Feb. 1776, C.O. 5/77; Chester to Germain, 28 June 1776, C.O. 5/592.
3. Lt. John Cambel to Earl of Dartmouth, May 1774, C.O. 5/592.
4. Dartmouth to Chester, 5 July 1775, C.O. 5/619.
5. Proclamation of Governor Peter Chester, 11 Nov. 1775, C.O. 5/592.

whom we have dependable records came from Georgia and South Carolina. The addition of such a strong contingent of loyalists to the original loyal inhabitants was an important factor in keeping West Florida attached to the British cause.[6]

When the noted botanist and traveler William Bartram made a tour of West Florida in 1778 he made no mention of the American Revolution. The fact that he failed to mention any evidence that the colony was aware and concerned that the rebellion existed, however, does not exclude that possibility. By 1776, the province was well aware of the Revolution, which had begun to have an impact on its life with the influx of loyalists into the newly proclaimed sanctuary. At this period, West Florida was not yet involved in fighting with the Americans and the war with Spain had not yet begun, but the officials in the colony keenly felt that the possibility of such a war existed. From the outbreak of hostilities at Lexington in 1775 until early 1778, West Florida was threatened only by the capture of ships leaving West Florida ports by American privateers and by constant rumors of rebel invasions. While the war scares amounted to little, relations with the Spanish in neighboring Louisiana continued to worsen. Distrust and suspicion characterized relations of British West Florida and Spanish Louisiana. These feelings were not unwarranted as almost from the establishment of the colony, the British in West Florida plotted to gain possession of New Orleans. In turn, the Spanish in Louisiana began aiding the rebellious colonists early in the American Revolution and would continue to do so, and ultimately would enter the war as a non-ally.[7]

The long-threatened invasion of West Florida occurred in 1778 as the American Revolution finally reached the colony. Acting under a commission of the Commerce Committee of the Continental Congress, Captain James Willing—a former resident of West Florida—forcefully brought the rebellion to the inhabitants of the

6. For a full discussion of the loyalists in West Florida, see chap. 10 of Starr, "Tories, Dons, and Rebels," pp. 372–99. The statistics in this chapter have been revised in my book of the same title.

7. Other than the raid of James Willing, the two main American ventures down the Mississippi River to New Orleans before the outbreak of the Anglo-Spanish War in 1779, were attempts to gain aid from the Spanish. In the summer and fall of 1776, a force of Virginians under Captain George Gibson succeeded in obtaining gunpower from the Spaniards, while a similar venture in 1778 led by Colonel David Rogers was in vain. Starr, "Tories, Dons, and Rebels," pp. 112–17, 130–33.

British frontier outpost. After leaving Fort Pitt on January 10, 1778, in the armed boat *Rattletrap*, Willing's force of about thirty volunteers increased on the trip down the Ohio and Mississippi to over one hundred men. Moving swiftly on the swollen rivers, the small group of Americans completely surprised and captured Natchez but apparently inflicted few injuries and did little damage to the property of the settlers. Below Natchez, however, Willing's tactics changed rapidly as he and his "body of banditti"[8] began a raid of plundering and destruction in the sparsely settled region.

Briefly and for the first time, the original inhabitants of West Florida faced the decision of remaining loyal to England or of joining the rebel cause. There was uncertainty in the minds of the confused residents as they went through the same difficult procedure of determining priorities which the loyalists of the colonies in rebellion had already done. The American Revolution in West Florida, however, ended almost as quickly as it had begun. Once Willing's raid was over and he left New Orleans, the revolt was at an end. The American excursion under a compelling but impulsive leader was more detrimental than helpful to the rebellious colonies. The raid did manage to interrupt briefly the flow of supplies from the Mississippi to Pensacola and the West Indies.

Probably the most important result of "the late rascally transaction of Mr. Willing,"[9] however, was a change in attitude by the British on the Mississippi. Before the expedition most of the residents were either neutral or pro-American in sentiment. After the American raid, however, intense loyalist sentiment developed as the settlers deprecated the plundering and devastation of the Americans. While many of the inhabitants must have agreed with William Dunbar that "twould be a prostitution of the name of Americans to honor them [Willing's party] with such an appelation,"[10] the depredations caused by an expedition sent down the Mississippi with a commission from Congress drove Floridians to hold a firmer allegiance to the British Crown, whose forces could protect them

8. Gov. Peter Chester to [?], 25 Mar. 1778, C.O. 5/129. For a full discussion of Willing's raid, see chap. 3 of Starr, "Tories, Dons, and Rebels," pp. 141–210, and John Walton Caughey, "Willing's Expedition down the Mississippi, 1778," *Louisiana Historical Quarterly* 15 (1932):5–36.

9. John Stephenson to Patrick Morgan, 7 Apr. 1778, quoted in John Walton Caughey, *Bernardo de Gálvez in Louisiana, 1776–1783*, reprint ed. (Gretna, La., 1972), p. 142.

10. Eron Dunbar Rowland, ed., *Life, Letters and Papers of William Dunbar* (Jackson, Miss., 1930), p. 63.

against such free-booting activities. The huge drafts for supplies which Willing drew on Oliver Pollock, the American agent in New Orleans, also caused the almost total destruction of Pollock's credit and, consequently, of his usefulness to the American cause.

Despite the efforts of local militia units and the fact that naval and troop reinforcements had been sent to West Florida to oppose the Americans during and immediately after Willing's raid, the American invasion impressed upon the British officials the weak and defenseless state of West Florida. Before Willing's expedition, fewer than five hundred regulars were scattered around the province to provide protection. Following orders from Whitehall, on October 31, 1778, over twelve hundred Waldeckers and Pennsylvania and Maryland Loyalists sailed from New York for Pensacola under the command of Brigadier General John Campbell.[11] Arriving in Pensacola in early 1779, Campbell and the troops under his command had time to do little more than disembark and begin repairing the fortifications, when Spain and England declared war upon each other.

The outbreak of the Anglo-Spanish war marked the beginning of another phase of the history of British West Florida. While they were aware that a rebellion was still in progress to the north, the West Floridians faced the even greater and more direct threat from their Spanish neighbors. No longer was there any question as to where their loyalty should rest. War against Spain in 1779 was no different from war with Spain in 1762; traditional loyalties became dominant as the American Revolution became more and more remote. The colony faced two separate wars whose dates overlap, but in West Florida they were distinct wars against totally different enemies and required completely revamped loyalties.

Although Spain declared war on England in June 1779, word of the outbreak of hostilities did not reach West Florida until September 8. General Campbell immediately began preparations for an attack on New Orleans. In the meantime, however, news of the Spanish declaration of war had reached New Orleans in mid-August. There Bernardo de Gálvez, the ambitious thirty-year-old governor of Louisiana, already had prepared for such a contingency

11. "State of a Detachment of Troops under the Command of Brigr. Genl. Campbell, on their Passage from New York for Pensacola in West Florida. Kingston the 26th December 1778," C.O. 5/597. Waldeckers were German mercenary forces from the province of Waldeck.

Impact of the American Revolution / 19

in order to make himself "master of all the establishments which they [the British] have on the Mississippi and particularly Mobile and Pensacola."[12] After several delays, on the morning of August 27, 1779, Gálvez led a force of Spanish regulars, militia, free blacks and mulattoes, and Americans out of New Orleans for an attack on Manchac, the southernmost British settlement on the Mississippi. Gathering additional strength along the march from militia and Indians, Gálvez arrived at Manchac on September 6 with 1,427 men. The British commander at Manchac, Colonel Alexander Dickson, however, had received intelligence that the Spanish were approaching Manchac and had moved the main body of his force to a hastily constructed, but more tenable, earthen redoubt at Baton Rouge. With fewer than 500 men under Dickson's command on the entire Mississippi, the outcome of the campaign was never in doubt. After easily capturing Manchac, the Spanish marched on to Baton Rouge where on September 21, after a three-hour cannonade, Dickson proposed a truce. The terms of the Articles of Capitulation that Gálvez dictated to the British required Dickson to surrender his entire command on the Mississippi—including Natchez. Dickson reluctantly agreed to the surrender of Natchez, and Gálvez sent a captain and 50 men to take possession of Fort Panmure. Resigned to their situation, the British settlers submitted peacefully to Spanish control.[13]

In one short campaign Gálvez had captured the entire British force along the Mississippi and secured New Orleans against attack from British subjects on the Mississippi. With the western area of West Florida safely in the hands of the Spanish, Gálvez was now free to turn to the two remaining strongholds in the colony, Mobile and Pensacola.

After two months' preparation, Gálvez' force of 754 men and 12 vessels embarked at New Orleans on January 11, 1780, for the campaign against Mobile. Lack of adequate water at the mouth of the Mississippi, adverse winds, and a hurricane delayed the expedition, but on February 9, Gálvez' scattered fleet (some of whom had sailed as far east as the Perdido River) regrouped off the bar at Mobile Bay. Eleven days later 5 ships arrived from Havana with

12. Bernardo de Gálvez to José de Gálvez, 17 Aug. 1779, Admiralty Office 1/241. For an excellent biography of Gálvez' career in Louisiana, see Caughey, *Bernardo de Gálvez*.
13. For a full discussion of the campaigns against Baton Rouge, Mobile, and Pensacola, see Starr, "Tories, Dons, and Rebels," pp. 243–357.

20 / Eighteenth-Century Florida and the Revolution

1,412 men, equipment, and supplies. To oppose the Spaniards at Mobile, Lieutenant Governor Elias Durnford had under his command about 300 men, only a fraction of whom were regulars. Also sixty-three-year-old Fort Charlotte was in a sad state of disrepair; General Campbell reported that the fort and barracks were "almost a scene of ruin and desolation."[14]

After tending to the normal formalities of eighteenth-century warfare and some preliminary skirmishing, on March 12, 1780, the Spanish opened fire on Fort Charlotte. All day long an animated fire continued by both the Spanish and the English. The Spanish fire was effective as it dismounted two cannon (which were quickly replaced) and battered the walls until the attackers had opened two large breaches. The British cannon replied vigorously all day despite the hunger and fatigue from which the garrison was suffering. The artillerymen remained at their weapons until they ran out of ammunition. There were both cannon and ammunition in the arsenal, but not of the same caliber. Finally at sunset, Durnford hoisted the white flag asking for a truce. Two days later, on March 14, the formal surrender of Fort Charlotte took place. Slow-moving General Campbell, torn by indecision as to whether the Spanish planned to attack Mobile or Pensacola, had finally left Pensacola with a force of over five hundred regulars, militia, and Indians to support Durnford. Before the reinforcements arrived, however, Mobile had surrendered; consequently, Campbell returned to Pensacola with nothing accomplished and the loss of seven men.

One Spaniard who was present at the siege of Mobile did not believe their victory was of consequence. "The conquest of Mobile is to us of little importance, so that we may say that all we have done has been to endure much fatigue and put the king to much fruitless expense."[15] With the capitulation of Mobile, however, British West Florida was reduced to the district of Pensacola. Mobile could no longer serve as a source of supply for Pensacola, and all effective communication was cut off to the west of Mobile. The British control of the western Indians was in doubt as the Choctaws began turning against the British, and the loyalty of the Chickasaws was questionable. The "outpost of the plaza of Pen-

14. Campbell to Sir Henry Clinton, 10 Feb. 1779, C.O. 5/597.
15. Gaspar Francisco to Gabriel Montenego, 16 June 1780, Sir Henry Clinton Papers, William L. Clements Library, Ann Arbor, Michigan.

Impact of the American Revolution / 21

sacola"[16] had joined Manchac, Baton Rouge, and Natchez in the fold of conquered territory. Only Pensacola remained British.

Gálvez intended to lead an expedition against Pensacola immediately after Fort Charlotte's surrender, as the seizure of Pensacola was the ultimate aim of the Spanish conquests on the Gulf of Mexico. A swift campaign against Pensacola would take advantage of confusion in the town following Campbell's unsuccessful attempt to reinforce Mobile and would not allow time for the British to receive reinforcements or to improve their fortifications. Delays necessitated by Gálvez' need for army and naval reinforcements, internal disagreements and indecision among Spanish officials, and the vagaries of weather prevented the rapid movement that he desired, and it was nearly a year before the Spaniards began the investment of Pensacola.

In the meantime the British worked feverishly to prepare for the coming attack. With constant rumors of Spanish ship sightings, the Pensacola residents were on edge in anticipation of a Spanish landing. General Campbell also began to feel the pressure of constant vigilance, and tired of waiting for Gálvez to attack, he decided to take the initiative. On Sunday morning, January 7, 1781, a force of approximately eight hundred Waldeckers, regulars, provincials, and Indians attacked a Spanish outpost on the east side of Mobile Bay known as the Village of Mobile or Spanish Fort. The expedition was a disaster for the British, and they beat a hasty retreat back to Pensacola to argue over who was to blame for the defeat.

Also throughout the year between the battles at Mobile and Pensacola, Campbell determined that additional work was needed on the defenses of Pensacola, which after seventeen years of British possession were still in need of major repairs and renovation. Deciding that the old garrison fortress in the town could not be adequately defended, the commander ordered construction of Fort George on Gage Hill, 1,200 yards north of the existing fortress. In order to protect Fort George, he also directed the erection of the Queen's Redoubt on the northwest end of Gage Hill with the smaller Prince of Wales' Redoubt in between. To guard the entrance to the bay, seamen fabricated the Royal Navy Redoubt. To

16. José de Gálvez to Bernardo de Gálvez, 22 June 1780, quoted in Caughey, *Bernardo de Gálvez,* p. 186.

man these wood and sand fortifications, Campbell could call upon a polyglot force of only 1,736 to 1,836 men, including regulars, Waldeckers, provincials, Indians, militia, Negroes, and seamen. Without reinforcements, the prospects of facing over 8,000 Spanish and French troops were grim.

After a year's delay, Gálvez' force arrived off Santa Rosa Island on March 9, 1781, and the long-anticipated battle for Pensacola was about to begin. For the next two months the Spanish moved inside the bay, set up camp, and began construction of trenchworks that got progressively closer to Fort George and its redoubts. Minor skirmishes occurred as Campbell ordered out small parties to harass the Spanish as they continued their construction, but no major assault occurred. Finally, on May 1, the Spanish began bombardment of the British fortifications and the British responded. The heavy shelling continued until May 7, doing major damage to the fortifications but with neither side inflicting many casualties.

The eighth of May, 1781, began like so many of the preceding days. At 6:00 A.M. the British in the Queen's Redoubt began bombarding the Spanish again and the Spanish returned the fire with two howitzers from their redoubts. Between 8:30 and 9:00 one of the howitzer shells burst just outside the open door of the magazine where the British were obtaining powder. An explosion rocked the redoubt and, as Campbell reported, "in an instant reduced the body of the redoubt to a heap of rubbish. . . ," killing seventy-six and wounding twenty-four.[17] The Spanish soon seized what was left of the Queen's Redoubt, set up batteries and opened fire on the Prince of Wales' Redoubt. The British returned the fire, but the advanced redoubt held a commanding position, and thirty of the British defenders soon lay wounded. Realizing that he could hold out only a few days at the expense of many lives, at three o'clock Campbell ordered the white flag raised and proposed a truce. Twenty-four hours later the formal surrender took place.

With the surrender of Pensacola, Spain had captured all of West Florida, and she was likely to keep the province unless Britain recaptured it. Pensacola surrendered in May 1781, two years before the general peace settlement. These two years in West Florida were

---

17. Campbell to Clinton, 12 May 1781, British Headquarters' Papers (Carleton Papers or Lord Dorchester Papers; microfilm located at Florida State University), 9918, reel 27.

Impact of the American Revolution / 23

filled with intrigue and rebellion, while England, Spain, and the United States pondered the final disposition of the remote region.

The most notable event during these two years was the revolt in mid-1781 of the English settlers at Natchez against Spanish rule. Primarily a chapter in Spanish history, the revolt occurred in April and May when a group of British citizens at Natchez forced the capitulation of Fort Panmure. Their success was short-lived, however, for when word of the surrender of Pensacola reached Natchez, the rebels deemed it prudent to return the post to the Spanish.[18]

While the Natchez insurrection marked the end of open fighting against the Spanish in what was once British West Florida, it by no means ended British intrigue in the area. Throughout the remainder of the Anglo-Spanish war, and even after the conclusion of the war, many ex–West Floridians and others attempted to get England to retake West Florida as a haven for the loyalists. The loyalists' desire for land speculation, their wish to regain lands and possessions lost when Spain captured the province, and their plans to unite eventually British-held Canada and West Florida through the Ohio Valley as a check on the rebellious states all militated in favor of such a venture.

While there were several other proposals, the most ambitious and most advanced intrigue was that of Lord John Murray, the Earl of Dunmore. The ex-governor of Virginia advocated an attack on West Florida in order to provide a home for dispossessed and fleeing loyalists, to allow West Floridians to regain their homes and possessions, and not incidentally, to allow Dunmore to gain new lands for speculation to replace the four million acres he had lost in the Ohio Valley. Beginning in late 1781 and continuing throughout 1782 and 1783, Dunmore urged the adoption of his proposal, but the home government never embraced the scheme.[19]

The 1783 Anglo-American Treaty of Paris and the accompanying treaties among England, France, and Spain crushed any real chance of success for British intrigue in West Florida. Discussions of the negotiations concerning West Florida generally centered around the question of the "Separate Article," which was in the preliminary

18. The "Natchez Rebellion" is covered well by John W. Caughey in chap. 13 of his biography of Gálvez.
19. For a full discussion of Dunmore's intrigue, see J. Leitch Wright, Jr., "Lord Dunmore's Loyalist Asylum in the Floridas," *Florida Historical Quarterly* 49 (1971):370–79.

treaty of 1782 but was omitted from the definitive treaty of 1783.[20] While the confusion caused by this section of the treaty would continue until the Pinckney Treaty of 1795, a much more important question in relation to West Florida's role in the American Revolution remains to be fully explored; that is, what real difference did West Florida make in the treaties ending the American Revolution and the Anglo-Spanish War? Professor Cecil Johnson suggests that there is a "lack of documentary evidence showing a cause-and-effect relationship between the Spanish conquest of West Florida and its subsequent cession to Spain."[21] Despite the lack of documentary evidence, the fact that West Florida was in the hands of Spain while the negotiations were underway was influential in the peace settlement. As Professor Robert Rea points out in what he calls an "exploratory essay," "the plain fact was that Spain would be as unlikely to part with conquered West Florida as Britain was to part with unconquered Gibraltar."[22]

At the end of the American Revolution Britain's most pressing problem concerning West Florida was what to do with the loyalists whom the Spanish had evicted from the colony. When the war broke out, West Florida did not join the rebels but remained loyal to the Mother Country. Unfortunately, every major historian of the loyalists in America had ignored the loyal colony of West Florida. While some contemporaries questioned the loyalty of the West Floridians, arguing that there were "few persons fit to be trusted"[23] and "excepting the army and navy, the number of loyalists . . . is very small,"[24] the evidence strongly indicates that loyalty was the norm rather than the exception in the frontier colony.

20. A copy of the "Separate Article" is in Richard B. Morris, *The Peacemakers: The Great Powers and American Independence* (New York, 1965), p. 552, and Samuel Flagg Bemis, *The Diplomacy of the American Revolution* (Bloomington, Ind., 1957), p. 264.
21. Cecil Johnson, "West Florida Revisited," *Journal of Mississippi History* 28 (1966):130.
22. Robert R. Rea, "British West Florida: Stepchild of Diplomacy," in *Eighteenth-Century Florida and Its Borderlands*, ed. by Samuel Proctor (Gainesville, Fla., 1975), pp. 61, 76. See also J. Leitch Wright, Jr., *Anglo-Spanish Rivalry in North America* (Athens, Ga., 1971), pp. 132–33. The most recent and one of the best discussions of the diplomacy concerning West Florida is in J. Leitch Wright, Jr., *Florida in the American Revolution* (Gainesville, Fla., 1975), pp. 111–24.
23. John Stuart to Sir William Howe, 23 Aug. 1777, British Headquarters' Papers, 649, reel 2. For a full discussion of the loyalists in West Florida, see Starr, "Tories, Dons, and Rebels," pp. 372–99.
24. Robert Taitt to Thomas Browne, 23 May 1777, C.O. 5/558.

Sharing little in common with their loyal brethren in the rebellious colonies, West Floridians remained loyal because of such factors as their isolation, the fact that it was a colony of recent immigrants, skillful (and perhaps unscrupulous) management of the government by Governor Peter Chester, and the presence of a large number of troops in proportion to the population. Already a loyal colony, the strength of the loyalty of West Florida increased after November 1775 with the addition of loyalists fleeing from the colonies in rebellion to the haven proclaimed by Chester. Another key point in understanding the loyalty of the inhabitants is the fact that the colony became involved in a war with Spain. Once England and Spain declared war upon each other, the whole situation in West Florida changed. No longer were the colonists faced with the decision of loyalty to England or joining the Americans. The issue became one of loyalty, or of joining an ancient enemy. This important change placed the question of loyalty in a different light. While a few inhabitants may have harbored some desire to join the Americans, the thought of siding with the troops of "His Catholic Majesty" was an anathema.

As for the composition of the loyalists, the usual stereotype of office holders, clergy of the Anglican church, landowners, merchants—in general, the wealthy—did not hold true in West Florida. While it is true all of these types of men were present in the frontier colony and remained loyal, so did virtually everybody else even though they fit into none of these categories. Except briefly during Willing's raid, the inhabitants were never forced into the position of having to decide where their loyalties lay until the outbreak of war with Spain, and then the question was much easier to answer. It was easier to be a loyalist in West Florida than in the colonies in rebellion, as the heartrending decision of loyalty to the Mother Country or to the American soil never had to be made. If an inhabitant in West Florida simply made no decision, he was in fact a loyalist. The patriots had to do the converting, and in West Florida the change did not occur. If loyalty was the norm and the conversion process did not take place, the pre-1775 inhabitants remained loyal to the Mother Country by default.

One question remains to be answered. What happened to the loyalists after the Spanish conquest of the frontier province? While statistics are meager, they indicate that many of the British remained in the colony after the war and switched their allegiance.

The evidence suggests that a majority and perhaps as many as two-thirds of the loyalists remained. To do so was not inconsistent with action of loyalists in the original thirteen colonies, nor with the principles of loyalty. At the end of the Revolution throughout the colonies, many loyalists remained at their homes or returned to them when the opposition to their doing so was slight. Since West Florida was a "loyal" colony, and since the Spanish had little objection to the loyalists remaining, many of them simply did not move. Not only did many West Floridians remain in the colony, but large numbers of loyalists from other colonies (particularly East Florida) sought the protection of the Spanish government in West Florida. Governor Patrick Tonyn of East Florida reported in early 1784, for example, that four thousand inhabitants from East Florida were moving to the Mississippi.[25] Thus the loyalist haven that Dartmouth attempted to establish in 1775 and which Dunmore planned during the last years of the war became in part a reality. It was not the refuge under British control which Dartmouth and Dunmore envisioned, but it was, nevertheless, an asylum for the loyalists of West Florida and the other ex-British colonies.

The loyalists who left West Florida continued to suffer because of their loyalty. When the Commission for Enquiring into the Losses, Services, and Claims of the American Loyalists met, it excluded West Floridians from consideration except for damages arising out of Willing's raid. Certainly the decision of the commission is easy to understand. If it had granted compensation to West Floridians for their losses to Spain, England would at once have been saddled with debts arising from claims around the world because of the global conflicts in which she became involved. At the same time many West Florida loyalists suffered almost total destruction of their personal fortunes, and the failure of England to grant some kind of relief through direct compensation or an annual pension seems callous. The commission did grant small annual pensions amounting to £410 per year to eight West Floridians for property lost to the Americans during Willing's raid. For over thirty years the remainder of the West Florida loyalists continued to seek compensation or confirmation by the United States of their British land grants in West Florida, but by and large their efforts were in vain.

25. Quoted in Wilbur Henry Siebert, *Loyalists in East Florida, 1774 to 1785*, 2 vols. (DeLand, Fla., 1929), 1:156.

What, then, may be said of the importance of the American Revolution in West Florida? The defense of West Florida is an important chapter in British colonial policy during the Revolution. By reinforcing the colony, the British kept the Spanish from using their troops against the British troops in the rebellious colonies. Or as a disgusted General Campbell said shortly after the surrender of Pensacola, "What interpretation can the whole bear, but that it was considered no object of national concern, and left as a gewgaw to amuse and divert the ambition of Spain and prevent it from attending to objects of greater moment and importance."[26] Once the war was over and the negotiators were attempting to decide the fate of West Florida, had Spain not been in possession of West Florida, it is unlikely that Great Britain would have surrendered it to Spain. Historians have strongly documented the fact that Spain's ownership of West Florida facilitated American acquisition of the area later. The loyalists who settled in West Florida are an important part of the history of the American loyalists of the Revolution. Perhaps more important, however, is the fact that they proved the fertility of the soil on the Mississippi and consequently encouraged expansion into the Old Southwest. If England had retained West Florida, she would have been an obstacle to American expansion. With the weak control of Spain and the presence of large numbers of loyalists, who in time became pro-American, the new nation began achieving its manifest destiny long before J. L. O'Sullivan ever coined the phrase.

26. Campbell to Clinton, 21 May 1781, British Headquarters' Papers, 9919, reel 27.

Commentary

GEORGE C. ROGERS, JR.

THE papers that have been presented are solid, interesting, and suggestive. They attempt to probe the nature of loyalist sentiment in East and West Florida. Professor Leitch Wright suggests that the majority of the East Floridians were loyalists because the province had been dominated by the Scots, army officers, and placemen. Professor Barton Starr indicates that the persons residing in West Florida in 1776 did not have to face a decision one way or the other until very late in the war and by then, West Florida had become a haven for many of the loyalist refugees leaving Georgia and South Carolina. Thus West Florida was neutral first, loyalist second.

But the chief question, which neither paper ever successfully penetrates, is who were the people of the Floridas. Can one avoid, as Professor Wright says, lumping all persons together, seeing them simply as one group? Can one ever know enough of the lives of individuals so that life sketches can be assembled as pieces in a mosaic until the total picture emerges? This can be done now better than at any previous time. My work on the *Papers of Henry Laurens*[1] has convinced me that the scholar can come to know the individuals of these southeastern societies: the cooper, the sea captain, the slave, as well as the merchant, the planter, and the factor. While I was pursuing every facet of the South Carolina society in the 1760s I stumbled upon the best collection for the study of East Florida that has yet been revealed—the papers of James Grant,

1. *The Papers of Henry Laurens*, ed. George C. Rogers, Jr. and David R. Chesnutt, 5 vols. to date (Columbia, S.C., 1968–) (hereafter *HL Papers*).

Commentary / 29

governor of East Florida from 1763 to 1771. This collection is at Ballindalloch Castle in the north of Scotland on the River Spey in Banffshire. It is the property of Sir Ewan Macpherson-Grant.[2] The Scottish Record Office became aware of these papers in 1971; the calendar of the collection was only completed in the fall of 1974. Of the more than 700 bundles in the collection, 125 pertain either to South Carolina or to East Florida.

An examination of these letters and documents shows they contain valuable information and data about the people of East Florida and by inference the people of West Florida. The prime movers in each province were the Scots. There are some fascinating characters in the story of East Florida in the 1760s. The person that binds many of the events of these times together is Lord Adam Gordon, the fourth son of the second Duke of Gordon. He arrived in 1764 to post his regiment in the West Indies and then made a tour of Pensacola, St. Augustine, Charleston, and the northern colonies. After being handsomely entertained by Governor James Grant in St. Augustine, he spent the winter of 1764–65 in Charleston.[3] John Moultrie, who was Lord Adam's host in Charleston, confided to Grant on January 30, 1765, that after a number of drunken parties in Charleston, he, Lord Adam, and Captain Wallace of HMS *Tryal* had had to flee to the Moultrie plantation at Goose Creek "in order to cool a little." On March 23, 1765, Moultrie again wrote Grant saying that he should have written sooner, but "I was on pritty hot service with" Lord Adam.[4] Lord Adam on his way to the North stopped at Georgetown, South Carolina, to discuss indigo crops with Francis Kinloch.[5] In New York City at the time of the Stamp Act Congress, he talked to Thomas Lynch about ventures in East Florida.[6]

Colonel John Scott of the Twenty-sixth Regiment of Foot, who represented the Scottish boroughs in Parliament from 1754 to his death in 1777, visited St. Augustine in 1769. He was a celebrated

2. I am indebted to Mr. Daniel Littlefield of the Department of History, York College of the City University of New York, Jamaica, New York, for drawing my attention to this collection.
3. "Journal of an Officer who Travelled in America and the West Indies in 1764 and 1765," in *Travels in the American Colonies*, ed. Newton D. Mereness (New York, 1916), pp. 367–453.
4. John Moultrie to James Grant, 30 Jan., 23 Mar. 1765, Bundle 261, Ballindalloch Castle Muniments.
5. Lord Adam Gordon to James Grant, 15 Mar. 1765, Bundle 474, ibid.
6. Lord Adam Gordon to James Grant, 5 Oct. 1765, Bundle 483, ibid.

gambler who had gained a fortune estimated at £500,000 sterling. According to Lady Haden-Guest, "when his luck at play ever faltered, the phenomenon was considered worth recording."[7] Presumably Governor James Grant acted on that rule, for after he won a slave from Colonel Scott at cards, Grant named the slave "Scott."[8] When General Scott died in 1777, a friend noted that Scott's London club would go "into mourning on Thursday. The waiters are to have crepes round their arms and the dice to be black and the spots white, during the time of wearing weepers, and the dice box muffled."[9]

A book on the South, the Scots, and the American Revolution is well worth doing, with a premise that the Highland Scots were the principal loyalists during the Revolution.[10] By focusing on the Highland Scots one can tell the entire story of the Southeast from 1763 to the end of the American Revolution.

First, one would have to concentrate on the governors of the Floridas—James Grant of East Florida and George Johnstone of West Florida—both of whom were appointed in October 1763. Grant arrived in St. Augustine in the fall of 1764 and remained in the province until May 1771. Johnstone stayed until 1767.[11] John Stuart wrote James Grant on March 1, 1767, that Governor Johnstone of West Florida had returned home as his brother John Johnstone had arrived from India with a fortune of £300,000 sterling which needed managing.[12] Later, both George and John Johnstone secured seats in the House of Commons.

Grant was a Highland Scot; Johnstone a Lowland Scot. Around them grouped their Scottish friends, all of whom were seeking to make their fortunes. It is often asked, as indeed Professor Wright has done, why the Scots were so loyal to the Hanoverians during the American Revolution. The answer is quite simple and clear. The second half of the eighteenth century was the golden age of

7. Sir Lewis Namier and John Brooke, *The History of Parliament: The House of Commons, 1754–1790*, 3 vols. (New York, 1964), 3:413–14.
8. John Torrans to James Grant, 30 May 1769, Bundle 552, Ballindalloch Castle Muniments.
9. Namier and Brooke, *The House of Commons*, 3:413–14.
10. The reader should keep in mind that there are distinct differences between the Highland Scots, the Lowland Scots, and the Scotch-Irish.
11. For the careers of James Grant and George Johnstone see Namier and Brooke, *The House of Commons*, 2:529–31, 683–85.
12. John Stuart to James Grant, 1 Mar. 1767, Bundle 251, Ballindalloch Castle Muniments.

Scottish history—a period that brought a great upsurge in the energies of the people, producing vast wealth and a distinct cultural renaissance. The defeat at Culloden triggered this outburst of energy. What one overlooks is that the government in London tried to buy the support of the Scots in many ways. The Scottish members of Parliament generally supported the government in power; in return they and their friends received profit and privilege. The chance to exploit the Floridas was one of the avenues to profit and high position.

But before one can analyze this Scottish rapaciousness, the story of the failure of South Carolinians to exploit the potential of this southern region should be examined. Henry Laurens, Francis Kinloch, Thomas Lynch, John Moultrie, William Drayton, and others considered establishing themselves in Florida.[13] The plantation system was extended first into Georgia and then further south with the Altamaha grants of 1763. That movement was successful and Henry Laurens was the prime example of the enterprising planter. But was there the possibility of also extending the indigo plantation system into East Florida? Francis Kinloch, who had the greatest expertise in the planting and production of indigo, was considering such a move when he died in June 1767. Neither Laurens nor Lynch, both of whom knew how to produce the best grades of indigo, ever actually launched Florida plantations. Except for John Moultrie and William Drayton, no South Carolina planter really succeeded in transferring his operations that far south, and both Moultrie and Drayton received salaries from high public offices to sustain them in their attempts. Drayton later sold his Florida plantation; Moultrie, alone among the South Carolinians in Florida, became a loyalist.

The great speculation in Florida lands in the 1760s took place in London.[14] The president of the East Florida Society was Lord Adam Gordon, and its principal members were members of Parliament, army contractors, and Scotsmen. These men secured orders in council in London for 10,000-20,000-acre land tracts in the Floridas. Among those securing grants were the Duke of Buccleuch, the Earl of Cassillis, the Earl of Thanet, the Earl of Moira, the Earl

---

13. Bundles 254 (Kinloch), 261 (Moultrie), 263 (Drayton), 359 (Laurens), and Lynch is mentioned in Bundles 394, 491, ibid.
14. George C. Rogers, "The East Florida Society, 1766–1767," *Florida Historical Quarterly* 54 (April 1976):479–96.

of Egmont, the Earl of Tyrone, Lord Adam Gordon, Sir Alexander Grant, Charles Townshend, Richard Oswald, John Hamilton, Peter Taylor, and John Murray. In all there were 227.

According to the terms of these orders in council, each man had to find someone to lay out his lands in Florida, have them surveyed, and have the grant recorded in St. Augustine. Ultimately the land had to be settled by a specified number of white Protestants. It was the last stipulation that caused Dr. Andrew Turnbull and Dr. William Stork to become such important personages in Florida since they had access to willing immigrants from Europe. Dr. Stork had contacts with Germans, Dr. Turnbull with Greeks. Richard Oswald informed James Grant on June 1, 1767, that the continuation of the authority to ship rice directly to the ports south of Cape Finisterre would facilitate getting cheap conveyance for Greeks, French Protestants, and persons from southern Switzerland who were experienced in raising the products of southern climates.[15]

Dr. Stork was the prince of the agents, having twenty persons for whom he was trying to establish plantations. He did not succeed and died a frustrated man in August 1768. But the agents of these great land speculators were an important group, playing an influential role in the colony, and they can be identified. John Tucker secured Joseph Stout of Philadelphia as his agent.[16] The Earl of Egmont who held property on Amelia Island sent out James Jollie.[17] Patrick Tonyn and Francis Levett, his son-in-law who had long been resident at Leghorn, sent Alexander Gray;[18] Charles Townshend and Lord Dartmouth dispatched Thomas Wooldridge;[19] Richard Oswald and Peter Taylor employed James Penman and William Mackdougall, who had served with them in Germany;[20] Thomas Thoroton and the Earl of Cassillis sent Captain John Fair-

15. Ever since the days of James I members of the Greek Orthodox church were lumped with the Protestants rather than with the Roman Catholics. For Oswald's letter see Bundle 295, Ballindalloch Castle Muniments.
16. Spencer Man to James Grant, 2 Sept. 1768, Bundle 412, ibid.
17. The Earl of Egmont dismissed James Jollie in 1769. Earl of Egmont to James Grant, 27 Oct. 1769, Bundle 264, ibid.
18. Patrick Tonyn to James Grant, 9 July 1767, Bundle 253, ibid.
19. Charles Townshend to James Grant, 19 Nov. 1766, Bundle 253, ibid.; Charles Loch Mowat, *East Florida as a British Province, 1763–1784* (Berkeley, Calif., 1943), p. 20.
20. Peter Taylor to James Grant, 16 Sept. 1766, Bundle 491, Ballindalloch Castle Muniments; *HL Papers*, 5:228.

Commentary / 33

lamb;[21] the Earl of Moira and the Earl of Tyrone had Charles Bernard;[22] William Elliott hired John Ross;[23] and David Yeats served Governor Grant from 1771 to 1784.[24] This group can be studied in great detail by examining the correspondence in the Grant papers. Each of these land speculators wrote to Governor Grant, and their letters have been preserved.[25]

Some of these agents came out in great style. Wooldridge arrived in Charleston in 1767 with a landau and two fine horses, although he was not to succeed in his ventures.[26] On November 1, 1774, the Reverend John Forbes informed Grant by letter of the progress of each of these attempts to operate plantations in East Florida.[27] As agents they would naturally have been allied with their masters in England and thus would have become loyalists. But the South Carolina gentry did not care for the land speculators. As Henry Laurens helped James Penman, Alexander Gray, and other agents, they would be torn in their loyalties between England and South Carolina.

Professor Wright states in his paper that "Few single white females" came to Florida. One can, however, through the letters of Sir Alexander Grant, get a glimpse of one group of young women. Sir Alexander was head of a London charitable institution, Magdalen House, which was a home for "reformed Penitents." Sir Alexander wrote "They are not Virgins 'tis true," but he informed Grant that at a recent meeting the board had decided to send with Dr. Stork four young women who had been chosen from the middle ranks. These four did arrive with Stork in the *Aurora* in the summer of 1767.[28]

Of those who came to New Smyrna with Dr. Turnbull more is known including the facts surrounding their revolt in the fall of

21. Earl of Cassillis to James Grant, 8 Apr. 1769; Thomas Thoroton to James Grant, 5 Sept. 1767, Bundle 412, Ballindalloch Castle Muniments.
22. Earl of Moira to James Grant, 20 Oct. 1767, Bundle 552; John Beresford to James Grant, 12 July 1767, Bundle 394, ibid.
23. William Elliott to James Grant, 15 June 1767, Bundle 264, ibid.
24. Bundle 250, ibid.
25. My article "The Papers of James Grant of Ballindalloch Castle, Scotland" was published in the *South Carolina Historical Magazine* 77 (July 1977): 145–60.
26. Andrew Turnbull to James Grant, 27 Jan. 1767, Bundle 253, Ballindalloch Castle Muniments.
27. Bundle 481, ibid.
28. Sir Alexander Grant to James Grant, 17, 19 June 1767, Bundle 402, ibid.

34 / Eighteenth-Century Florida and the Revolution

1768 and their later abandonment of that settlement.[29] Thus there were serious elements of discontent in East Florida. Yet, as both Wright and Starr have pointed out, St. Augustine and Pensacola were important military posts to which the army had withdrawn in the late 1760s. According to Wright, one-twentieth of the troops in America were at St. Augustine. Troops were moved from South Carolina to East Florida; thus the officers of these regiments, many of whom were either Scots or Swiss, like Prevost and Haldimand, became the primary maintainers of order. When Grant left in May 1771, the military men thanked him for his leadership.[30]

One statement made by Professor Wright is a matter of contention. If there were no Samuel Adamses or Patrick Henrys in East Florida, there was a Sons of Liberty movement. When James Grant left St. Augustine in May 1771 to take up his inheritance of Ballindalloch Castle, he was addressed by various groups in St. Augustine upon his departure: planters, members of the royal council, military men, and Masons. Their addresses were printed in the *General Gazette* in Charleston which was owned by Robert Wells from Dumfries in Scotland.[31] However, as John Moultrie assumed the role of lieutenant governor, a group of bolder men opposed to the Scottish faction presented an address to him in which they urged a different course from that taken by his predecessor, James Grant. They asked for the calling of an assembly, for the popular forms of government. This address, published by Peter Timothy in the *South-Carolina Gazette*, was signed by thirty-eight persons.[32] This is a longer list than the Sons of Liberty of Charleston.[33] A comparison of these names against De Brahm's census list of 1771 reveals twenty-seven who can be identified: six were storekeepers, four were carpenters, four were pilots or mariners, three were traders, or "livers in town," three were innkeepers, and only two were planters, and one each was a cooper, a mason, a haberdasher, an

29. E. P. Panagopoulos, *New Smyrna: An Eighteenth Century Greek Odyssey* (Gainesville, Fla., 1966).
30. *South Carolina and American General Gazette*, 20 May 1771.
31. Ibid., 13, 20 May 1771.
32. *South-Carolina Gazette*, 23 May 1771. Someone, probably John Moultrie, sent a clipping of this document from this issue to Grant. Bundle 278, Ballindalloch Castle Muniments.
33. Sketches of the twenty-six Charleston Sons of Liberty can be found in Joseph Johnson, *Traditions and Reminiscences Chiefly of the American Revolution in the South* (Charleston, S.C., 1851), pp. 27–36. For suggested additions to this list see *HL Papers*, 5:27n.

Commentary / 35

overseer, and an attorney at law.[34] This group belonged to the mechanic class in St. Augustine, a similar group to that which followed Christopher Gadsden in Charleston. William Collins, the lawyer, who had arrived with Dr. Stork in 1767, may have been the leader.[35] William Drayton wrote James Grant on May 13, 1771, that Edmund Grey, William Collins, and James Jollie were "a respectable triumvirate, figure away on every Post & Corner of the Town." Collins, who had presented the petition to Moultrie, may have been the author of the document asking for self-government. William Wilson, Thomas Stone, and Adam Bachop went with Collins to see Lieutenant Governor Moultrie.[36] Spencer Man notified Grant on September 1, 1771, that Stone and Wilson had not been so violent recently. "I believe Bachop's death has broke that party."[37] Of Adam Bachop and of Josiah Warner, who were pilots, one learns much from the Henry Laurens papers. An almost complete story about Bachop could be detailed. John Moultrie wrote Grant on December 13, 1764, praising Bachop as "a very sober honest man, in the highest degree obligeing, & seems a good Sailor, I am sure a very carefull one, & a very active one."[38] He served both Henry Laurens and James Grant for many years on the St. Augustine–Charleston run as master of the pilot boat *East Florida*.[39] Bachop drowned in August 1771, just ten days after his marriage.[40] Thus one can begin to probe the structure of society in Florida at the time. Although this protest of the St. Augustine mechanics failed, it did affect the power of the Scottish faction.

Later, when William Drayton and Andrew Turnbull had their disagreement with John Moultrie and Patrick Tonyn, there was a group that Drayton and Turnbull could reach out to for support. The Reverend John Forbes believed that "Drayton may wish to make a tool of William Collins."[41] Drayton and Jonathan Bryan were hoping on the eve of the American Revolution to secure con-

34. *De Brahm's Report of the General Survey in the Southern District of North America*, ed. Louis De Vorsey, Jr. (Columbia, S.C., 1971), pp. 180–86.
35. List of Passengers brought out by Dr. Stork in the *Aurora*, Bundle 412, Ballindalloch Castle Muniments.
36. William Drayton to James Grant, 13 May 1771, Bundle 297, ibid.
37. Spencer Man to James Grant, 1 Sept. 1771, Bundle 552, ibid.
38. John Moultrie to James Grant, 13 Dec. 1764, Bundle 261, ibid.
39. *HL Papers*, 4:483; 5:566.
40. James Penman to James Grant, 11 Aug. 1771, Bundle 491, Ballindalloch Castle Muniments.
41. John Forbes to James Grant, 23 Aug. 1773, Bundle 369, ibid.

trol of millions of acres of land around Apalache.[42] This is much like William Henry Drayton's attempt to get control of the Catawba Indian reservation in South Carolina. The fact that these attempts were blocked by royal officials may be the reason that both Draytons (they were first cousins) became patriots rather than loyalists.[43] William Drayton's motives are more difficult to fathom. He did go to England and lived in Wales until the end of the war.[44]

It might be possible by using the James Grant papers in conjunction with the Henry Laurens papers to tell the story of the introduction of slaves into East Florida. John Graham of Savannah was the merchant who transshipped many slaves to East Florida, particularly during the period when importation into South Carolina was cut off.[45] Richard Oswald asked Grant on February 19, 1768, if Negroes should not be substituted for Protestant settlers in the securing of land grants.[46]

The story of the Carlisle Peace Commission of 1778 might be examined in the light of Florida history. Henry Laurens was president of the Continental Congress during the summer of 1778 at the time of the mission. George Johnstone was one of the commissioners who accompanied Lord Carlisle. Behind the scenes was Richard Oswald writing letters to his former business associate Henry Laurens. The connections established in the development of the Floridas might be useful in bringing an end to the conflict.[47] Since Laurens was one of the five persons appointed by Congress to make peace with Great Britain and Oswald was one of the British negotiators, one wonders how their Florida associations affected the negotiations.

Professor Starr in his paper raises the important question of why Florida was retroceded to Spain in 1783. The obvious fact was that the Spaniards under Bernardo de Gálvez had captured Pensacola

42. John Moultrie to James Grant, 23 Dec. 1774, Bundle 521, ibid.
43. For William Henry Drayton's interest in the Catawba lands see William M. Dabney and Marion Dargan, *William Henry Drayton & the American Revolution* (Albuquerque, N.Mex., 1962), pp. 40–44.
44. George C. Rogers, Jr., *Evolution of a Federalist, William Loughton Smith of Charleston (1758–1812)* (Columbia, S.C., 1962), pp. 94–96.
45. John Graham to James Grant, 11 Sept. 1769, Bundle 401, Ballindalloch Castle Muniments.
46. Richard Oswald to James Grant, 19 Feb. 1768, Bundle 295, ibid.
47. R. F. A. Fabel, professor of history, Auburn University, who is writing a biography of George Johnstone, commented during the discussion that Johnstone did indeed try to make use of the connections established while he was in West Florida.

in May 1781. The Spaniards wished to hold on to West Florida as long as the British held on to Gibraltar. Of what importance was the Separate Article which was in the temporary treaty of peace but was not in the definitive treaty? The Separate Article was signed by both Laurens and Oswald along with Benjamin Franklin, John Adams, and John Jay. Were the Floridas needed as places of refuge for loyalists? John Murray, Lord Dunmore, had such a scheme for West Florida. Even though the Floridas were returned to Spain, many loyalists remained in the territory. Professor Starr explained why they stayed on in West Florida, but one might wonder more about Don Juan McQueen, Zephaniah Kingsley, and the Swiss career officer Francis Philip Fatio in East Florida. If the loyalists found it easy to stay on in Florida, why did so many Floridians end up in South Carolina after the war? Dr. Andrew Turnbull, Elihu Hall Bay, John Bowman, and George Lockey are examples.

There can be no doubt that Florida became a base for raids against Georgia and South Carolina during the American Revolution. The career of Thomas Brown is a fine example of this.[48] But the novels and historical writings of William Gilmore Simms might provide additional useful evidence. In his novel *Joscelyn*, Simms identified the loyalists as Scots.[49] In other novels he spoke often of gangs of Florida raiders. Professor Wright in his fine recent study, *Britain and the American Frontier, 1783–1815*,[50] has provided us with the framework for our future work. We must look at the pressures on the perimeters of the thirteen colonies, as well as the actions at Lexington and Concord and at Yorktown.

48. J. Leitch Wright, *Florida in the American Revolution* (Gainesville, Fla., 1975), pp. 23, 32, 36, 39, 40, 55, 56, 58.

49. *The Writings of William Gilmore Simms, Centennial Edition, Volume XVI. Joscelyn: A Tale of the Revolution*, introduction and explanatory notes by Stephen E. Meats. Text established by Keen Butterworth (Columbia, S.C., 1975).

50. J. Leitch Wright, *Britain and the American Frontier, 1783–1815* (Athens, Ga., 1975).

The Southern Contribution:

A Balance Sheet on the War

for Independence

ROBERT A. RUTLAND

A STROLL across the historic bridge at Concord or a migration to the Bunker Hill monument will become a routine pilgrimage in this year of our Lord 1976, as Americans pay homage to the embattled farmers, the men who waited until they saw the whites of British eyes, and the Minuteman immortalized by Daniel Chester French, a native of Exeter, New Hampshire. During the past few years we have been assailed by reports of a reenacted Boston Tea Party, a make-believe Boston Massacre, and unless we are very lucky indeed we will witness, in living color, a reenactment of the moment when Captain Parker's men stood their ground, and someone (we shall never know who and by now no one cares) fired that famous first shot. Orators keep telling us that first volley is still reverberating around the world. But notice the New England ring to all these events. And on April 19, as has been the custom for over one hundred years, the Boston schoolchildren will not worry about busing because that is Patriot's Day—a holiday more fabulous in Massachusetts than the anticlimactic Fourth of July. On the other hand, no Virginians take a day of rest on another nineteenth, October 19, to celebrate the final event of the great drama when Cornwallis surrendered at Yorktown—on southern soil to an army led by a southerner after leveling what had once been a little gem of a city, destroying in the process the home of Thomas Nelson, the selfless southerner who at the start of the war was rich and who died in penury shortly after it ended. For nearly two hundred years now that day has passed by almost unnoticed.

Yes, there was great talk of sacrifice and the spirit of 1776, but it seems to me that much of the rhetoric was generated on behalf of the notion that the Revolution was a northern-inspired event, essentially brought to fruition through the sacrifice of northern blood and treasure. Generations of our countrymen have heard Longfellow's words and trooped across Lexington green in pursuit of a glimpse of the glory of April 1775. And then there is Valley Forge with the stained glass windows depicting Washington kneeling in prayer in northern snow. And in upstate New York they still sing the praises of Herkimer, belittle Arnold, and speak of Saratoga as the turning point of the war. But consider that in 1777 the good news from Saratoga caused John Adams to exult that "one Cause" of the jubilation ought to be "that the Glory of turning the Tide of Arms, is not immediately due to the Commander in Chief, nor to southern Troops. If it had been, Idolatry, and Adulation would have been unbounded; so excessive as to endanger our Liberties, for what I know Now [is that] we can allow a certain Citizen to be wise, virtuous and good, without thinking him a Deity or a saviour."[1] Sour grapes, perhaps, but in a sense Adams was delivering tit for tat. We can recall that Washington—the "certain citizen" of Adam's jealous outburst—had held in scorn many of the New Englanders he dealt with at Cambridge in 1775. After Bunker Hill, Washington had told his kinsman in Virginia that he was surrounded by "the most indifferent kind of People I ever saw. I have already broke one Colo. and five Captains for Cowardice and for drawing more Pay and Provisions than they had Men in their Companies."[2] Not only were they crooks, but they were cowardly crooks. "There is two more Colos, now under arrest," Washington continued, "and to be tried for the same offences; in short they are by no means such Troops, in any respect, as you are led to believe of them from the accts. published." Washington was disenchanted by the variance between the reported troops extolled in Isaiah Thomas's *Massachusetts Spy* and the real army he was trying to lead. "I dare say the men would fight very well (if properly Officered) although they are an exceeding dirty and nasty people." Surrounded by Yankees, Washington felt that with proper leader-

1. L. H. Butterfield et al., eds., *The Book of Abigail and John* (Cambridge, Mass., 1975), p. 197.
2. George Washington to Lund Washington, 20 August 1775, John C. Fitzpatrick, ed., *The Writings of George Washington, from the Original Sources, 1745–1799*, 39 vols. (Washington, 1931–44), 3:433.

ship the battle at Breed's or Bunker's Hill might have turned out quite differently, and he was not indifferent to the first instances of Americans wilting in the face of enemy fire. "It was for their behavior on that occasion that the above Officers were broke," he concluded, "for I never spared one that was accused of Cowardice but brot 'em to immediate Tryal."

Thus we see, from the top rung of leadership in the Revolution, a jealousy based on sectional bias, an anger over the propaganda that made heroes out of sunshine patriots, a brooding contempt of the southerner for his northern comrades-in-arms, and Adams' backlash of discontent surfacing when an American victory broke a string of embarrassing losses. It would be wrong, however, to close the books on sectional contributions and jealousies without a search for evidence in counting houses as well as in company recruiting rolls. (It is too easy to pass off Adams' jealous assessment of Washington's greatness as based on wealth, height, and pride. In "Virginia geese are all swans" he told Benjamin Rush when asked to account for Washington's greatness.)[3]

Can we say of the Revolution that it was a northerner's war, but a southerner's fight? Perhaps, but before making such a claim we need a balance sheet that goes beyond Yorktown to see what came out of the experience which we are now pleased to call the War of Independence.

Insofar as the movement for independence goes, we must credit the South with the initiative in taking the step which timid men in Philadelphia and New York feared. Was John Adams merely feeding southern vanity when he assured Patrick Henry that the Congress looked to his state for examples? Richard Henry Lee, following the orders from the Virginia convention, took the fateful stride on June 7, 1776. To his wife, Adams was saying: "As to Declarations of Independency, be patient." He counseled Abigail, "Read our Privateering Laws, and our Commercial Laws. What signifies a Word."[4] Everything, it seemed, for after much hemming and hawing Lee called for the question. From below the Mason-Dixon line, only South Carolina hesitated; above it New York, Pennsylvania, and Delaware were unready. After an overnight pondering, the delegates voted again and Lee's motion passed, twelve to none.

3. Adams to Rush, 11 Nov. 1807, John A. Schutz and Douglass Adair, eds., *The Spur of Fame* (San Marino, Calif., 1966), p. 98.
4. Butterfield, *Book of Abigail and John*, p. 122.

When the matter went to a committee for proper phrasing, Adams again deferred to a southerner. When called upon to decide, the more likely prospect of a halter than a halo had deterred the New Yorkers and left a few Pennsylvanians queasy (three out of seven signed). Meanwhile, Virginia had on May 15 taken itself irrevocably out of the British Empire by its resolutions regarding independence, and by June 29 for all practical purposes Virginia was operating as an independent commonwealth, an example which shook the complacency of a whole train of states within the next twelve months and by imitation flattered the sensibilities of George Mason, Thomas Jefferson, James Madison, and the other slave-owning planters who were eager to talk about freedom. By the time the northern colonies proved themselves ready to become states, they found all the ideological questions already worked out for them by these landed aristocrats who were willing to become republicans, propounding constitutions and forms of government with explicit curbs on the powers of government born out of their experience. The paradox of the Virginia experience in the spring and summer of 1776 was that these aristocratic planters sought popular sanction for their actions. "Nothing has been done without the Approbation of the People," George Mason boasted in 1778, "the People, who have indeed out run their Leaders; so that no capital Measure hath been adopted, until they called loudly for it. . . . To us upon the Spot, who have seen Step by Step, the progress of this great Contest, who know the defenceless State of America in the Beginning, & the numberless Difficultys we have had to struggle with, taking a retrospective view of what is passed, we seem to have been treading upon enchanted Ground."[5] Of course, Mason's enchanted soil was southern soil, and by 1778—for this was a year when the army's fortunes sank—the South was thereafter destined to be the main battleground to determine whether all of Mason's hyperbole was ever to be justified. The French came into the war, but late in 1778 Savannah fell and in an ill-advised effort to retake the Georgia port 1,100 Americans died while the entrenched British suffered but few casualties. The threat to Georgia brought relief to the North, as the British abandoned their only stronghold outside of New York City at Newport, Rhode Island, and decided to conquer the South, destroy the American armies, and end the war.

5. Robert A. Rutland, ed., *The Papers of George Mason*, 3 vols. (Chapel Hill, N.C., 1970), 1:436.

The opening scenes in 1780 seemed to prove Lord George Germain's fondest expectations. He prayed that loyalist troops would join with the king's armies in a sweep that would prove the futility of further resistance. New Englander Benjamin Lincoln, called to command at Charleston, apparently felt pressure as the only northerner in the American force, and perhaps to avoid the political overtones of a southern surrender by a Yankee general, he blundered into a trap and ordered his men ready for battle. The outcome was total failure and the surrender of 5,500 men, 300 artillery pieces, two frigates, and hundreds of barrels of military stores. It was a disaster almost without parallel in the short history of the American army—greater than Burgoyne's humiliation at Saratoga and like the fiasco at Fort Washington in 1776 a distinct blow to southerners— 2,818 prisoners being lost in the New York surrender and a large share of them from the South, many destined to die in prison ships while their families in Maryland, North Carolina, and Virginia prayed for news of exchanges or paroles that never came, or came too late. So the southerners were paying a bitter price for their ticket out of the British Empire, and to many observers in New York and London, Charleston looked like the last phase of the war. As a matter of fact, Marshall Smelser reminds us, Charleston's loss can "be matched in the history of United States arms only by Julius White's surrender at Harper's Ferry in 1862, the Bataan debacle of 1942, and the surrender of the 106th Division in 1944."[6]

Of course we know that this was the darkest hour that preceded a terrible but tempering campaign under Cornwallis. The bloody road that Cornwallis followed to Yorktown started on an isolated South Carolina beach on a cold spring day in 1780 as the English peer set out to end the stalemate which was turning both Parliament and the Continental Congress into hotboxes of frustration and faction. The fleet of ninety ships and 9,000 men which sailed out of New York for Charleston bore in reality the last hope of the British, but in this war of attrition time then seemed on their side. Lincoln's capture was celebrated in London as the beginning of the end—as indeed it was—but the end of what? It was the end of dreams of loyalist uprisings, the end of indecisive skirmishes and wasted opportunities. At Camden the rout of Gates' army was highlighted by Gates' mad dash for the safety of a not-so-nearby North

6. Marshall Smelser, *The Winning of Independence* (Chicago, 1972), p. 270.

Carolina retreat, but at Kings Mountain the British learned that the dream of loyalist support was a chimera as the bloody fighting saw 1,100 Anglo-Americans and their British comrades perish and made the southern Generals Marion, Sumter, and Pickens anxious to show their mettle, which was something Nathanael Greene also needed to prove, after he relieved Gates. In essence these were southern soldiers fighting under a northern general on the red trail to Yorktown, and Greene must have felt some pressure owing to his background as a Rhode Island blacksmith and former Quaker turned general, now leading tobacco-chewing yeoman farmers and planters' sons. (He would emigrate to Georgia after the war and become a planter himself.)

Greene avoided the British traps, and in the meantime the South had another blow as the traitorous Arnold, his pockets lined with at least twelve pieces of silver, had commanded a British task force that swept up the Virginia peninsula and left a stain that is still not removed. Arnold's forces met little opposition and forced their way into the suburbs of the little capital at Richmond, destroyed the Westham Ironworks, and fell on the archives of the infant commonwealth. The state papers of Virginia were strewn about and burned, and so history was ground into the ashes of the Richmond bonfires which have left huge gaps in our knowledge of how the largest colony-turned-state conducted its affairs between 1775 and 1780. No other state suffered such indignities or felt the brunt of Arnold's treachery so much as Virginia.

Understandably, an important group of Virginians looked at the scenes of desolation and believed that they had been let down by their northern brethren. In the state legislature John Taylor of Carolina drafted a protest which was intended to be forwarded to the Virginia delegation in Congress to show the lopsidedness of the states' ardor for the war effort. The report scored the northerners "who in times of their own need, used the affectionate appellation of Brethren, but [who] appear now to have forgotten the duties of such a relationship. . . . 'Ere the war began we heard the cries of our brethren at Boston, and paid the tax due to distress. We accompanied our northern allies, during almost every progressive stride it made, where danger seemed to solicit our ardour. We bled with them at Quebeck, at Boston, at Harleam, at White Plains, at Fort Washington, at Brandywine, at Germantown, at Mud Island, at White Marsh, at Saratoga, at Monmouth and at Stony point. . . .

But when we came to look for our Northern allies, after we had thus exhausted our powers in their defense, when Carolina and Georgia became the theatre of war, they were not [to] be found."[7] The Virginia remonstrance claimed that southerners alone had carried the brunt of battle from Savannah through to Cowpens, and in March 1781 Taylor insisted that Virginia, "impoverished by defending the northern department, exhausted by the southern war, now finds the whole weight of it on her shoulders." Taylor blamed northern indifference to the South's burdens as shown by the failure to send money or supplies for their beleaguered brothers, with the consequence that "our only resource, is the wretched one of more paper money, in addition to enormous taxes, which are the more peculiarly distressing, as they must be collected whilst near 10,000 of our citizens exclusive of our regular troops, are in the field." Sagacious Edmund Pendleton told Madison, to whom the rough draft was sent, to consider the complaints as more Taylor's than the legislature's, but he added, "It may be not improper perhaps for Congress to pay some attention to the Sentiments, tho' you'l not publish the paper." So Madison, in the interests of national unity, apparently pocketed the protest without sharing its contents with the northerners for whom it was intended.

Neither Taylor nor Madison nor, for that matter, Washington himself could have foreseen the circumstances that soon sent American hopes soaring after months of near despair. We need not recount the triumphs and failures between Kings Mountain and Yorktown. Cowpens had been the classic battle, a military textbook situation, while Guilford Court House and Eutaw Springs were other measured steps on the weary road to victory. Then finally, the impossible happened, partly owing to British ineptitude and partly to the combination of French and American daring plus some luck of the draw. And so on October 19, Cornwallis was bottled up, abandoned to his fate, and what Rochambeau later called "the miracle of the blockade and capture of Cornwallis" occurred, with Washington as commander-in-chief in his native state on a battlefield only a few miles from the very place where the Virginia Convention had voted five years and five months earlier to break all bonds with England.

The story could not end there, although little fighting took place

7. Enclosure in John Taylor's hand, with Edmund Pendleton to James Madison, 26 March 1781 Rives Collection, University of Virginia Library.

thereafter and that notable for the totally useless loss of the promising young William Washington. Thousands of militiamen and regulars, mainly from Maryland, Virginia, and North Carolina, returned to their homes and huzzahed the name of Washington to the last echo when he met Congress in Annapolis and turned in his sword, bound so he thought for the sweet retirement of Mount Vernon under his own vine and fig tree.

Only the military phase of the Revolution had ended, however, and thus it seemed to be left up to the South to cement the victory. Certainly the initiative for a restructured national government was the South's doing. From the moment of the Mount Vernon Compact in 1785 on through the Annapolis Convention to the federal gathering in Philadelphia in 1787 it was the fine hand of either Mason or Madison or their colleagues in the Virginia House of Delegates always leading the way. There was no greater nationalist in all the Union than Washington, unless perhaps it was Madison, as these southerners eschewed sectional leanings to appeal to their fellow southerners for the magnanimity needed to make the Revolution a political as well as a military success. The Virginia Plan kept the Philadelphia convention on a course of republican commitment, and while doing so the delegates heard Madison frankly state that "it seemed now to be pretty well understood that the real difference of interest lay, not between the large & small but between the N. & Southern States. The institution of slavery & its consequences formed the line of discrimination."[8] He went on to imply that even though there were five southern states overbalanced by eight northern ones, he was willing to submerge sectional concerns for the greater good of a virile republic capable of demonstrating the blessings of self-government to a skeptical world. The Constitution which resulted from their deliberations was full of sectional concessions, but even so eloquent a northerner as Oliver Ellsworth believed that in time slavery would not be a speck on the American scene, and the New Englanders reasoned that they could grow strong by shipping southern produce to markets stretching from Canton to Calais.

The Constitution had barely been in operation when a sectional clash opened old wounds, however, and in the halls of Congress the question of who had done their fair share during the fighting phases

8. James Madison, *Notes of Debates in the Federal Convention of 1787* (Athens, Ohio, 1966), p. 295.

of the war caused tempers to flair anew. In justice we must allow that the northerners also believed they had borne more than their share of the wartime burdens, and as Samuel A. Otis complained late in 1788, "the great disproportion of men we had in the field, the astonishing loss by old money, and want of alertness in bringing forward accounts . . . will hang like a mill stone about the neck of Massachusetts for ages."[9] The eight northern states had about eleven million dollars worth of unpaid war debts, about the same amount facing the southern taxpayers. Massachusetts and South Carolina, with four million each, had the lion's (or some would have said, and did say, the hog's) share. But listen to Congressman Jackson of Georgia argue, when the fight over assumption of state debts reached a fever pitch. Jackson said he "came from a State which had suffered the most of any in the Union; where there was no place, no corner but where the British arms had been carried; where the families had been wholly driven off, and their property had been totally destroyed . . . where what the British had left the army had taken to subsist on, and not a certificate had been given in numerous instances. . . . Would it be justice, after all these losses, & after this voluntary contribution, to put our hands again in their pockets, and say, you must pay the debts of Massachusetts and South Carolina?"[10]

Aedaneus Burke of South Carolina had a different view. There was not a road in South Carolina, he said, "but has witnessed the ravages of war; plantations were destroyed, and the skeletons of houses, to this day, point out to the traveller the route of the British army . . . men, women and children murdered in cold blood, by the Indians and tories . . . now is it to be wondered at that she is not able to make exertions equal with other States, who have been generally in an undisturbed condition."[11] The South Carolina war debt had been "contracted in the common cause, in fighting the battles of the Union." The loss of fighting men in South Carolina had been so great, Burke insisted, "that there was not less than fourteen hundred widows in one county, at the close of the war. After all these things, to be left or be pressed down by the enor-

9. Samuel A. Otis to Nathan Dane, 29 October 1788, in *Letters of Members of the Continental Congress,* ed. Edmund C. Burnett, 8 vols. (Washington, 1921–36), 8:811.
10. Speech of 1 March 1790, *Annals of the Congress of the United States,* 1st Cong., 2d sess., p. 1431.
11. Ibid., p. 1416.

Southern Contribution to the War for Independence / 47

mous weight of taxes [to pay off the state war debts] is unreasonable and unjust."[12] Thanks, of course, to the lobbying of the investors of Boston, Philadelphia, and New York and their friend Mr. Hamilton, South Carolina's debt became the nation's debt. But in their moments of truth even some of the northerners who profited from the war could be candid. Stephen Higginson confessed that ordinary rules of prudence and good judgment had been allowed to slide during the Revolution. In 1790 he told Hamilton, "We have not yet got wholly rid of the habits contracted during the War, & do not manage our business with that industry & oeconomy, which must be adopted to carry [business forward] with advantage."[13] The passage of the Assumption bill, in my judgment, marked the end of the era that began in 1765 as a protest movement, became a war, and finally saw a nation emerge. The Funding Act had all the features of a gigantic pork-barrel bill, with something for everybody, but its passage consolidated more than the war debt, erasing, in the marketplace at least, all the contention about who had fought the most, bled the most, suffered the most. The Assumption bill told the nation that whatever the costs had been for independence, the price was not too high. If speculators made some huge profits, that could not be helped, for it settled the old scores of money owed and money lent, and placed in its compromise the national capital astride the eastern seaboard. For a rare moment, Washington was happy, Hamilton was happy, Jefferson was happy, and Madison was not too unhappy. The Union had been preserved and the Founding Fathers were ready to concede, as Robert Frost later told us, that one's life cannot be devoted to wondering how each cent is spent.

Fortunately, certain things were beyond all price or calculation of price. Most precious was the liberty, the liberty embodied in the daily actions of Americans, the first men who knew no ancient customs of privilege and birth but only the free route embodied in the documents written and speeches made, chiefly by southerners, from the time of Patrick Henry's bold defiance at Richmond to James Madison's genteel weaving of theoretical republicanism into a working plan of action at Philadelphia. Oblivious of the sour

12. Ibid., p. 1411.
13. Higginson to Hamilton, 20 May 1790, in *The Papers of Alexander Hamilton*, eds. Harold C. Syrett and Jacob E. Cooke, 22 vols. to date (New York, 1961–), 6:425.

note of slavery, they talked of freedom, for they knew its efficacy in their homes and churches, in their printing offices, and in their halls of state. Their concept of personal liberties involved a respect for the law and a belief that republicanism was best fostered when rooted in an agrarian society. These southern planters and farmers, proud and fiercely independent, thought they had dragged their northern brothers along into a new era of human history. Although they sometimes had lingering doubts about the costs, they believed that the balance sheet would in time prove that all mankind had benefited from the American Revolution. Whatever the cost, it had been worth the gamble, and "generations unborn" would be the beneficiaries of their commitment. During some heated debate at the Federal Convention, after Gouverneur Morris had made a blatantly sectional speech calling for limitations on newly admitted western states, Madison felt moved to a rebuttal. "If the Western people get the power in their hands," Morris said, "they will ruin the Atlantic interests."[14] This was too much for Madison, who wanted the West to come into the Union on equal terms just as men entered society on equal terms. "To reconcile the gentleman with himself it must be imagined that he determined the human character by the points of the compass," Madison said. "The truth was that all men having power ought to be distrusted to a certain degree."[15] This southerner had in capsule form expressed the philosophical undertone of the American Revolution: we cannot trust men individually, but we must trust mankind. In the keeping of accounts, surely the ledger shows that it is we who are indebted, indebted to the great southerners who above the din of battle gave the Revolution its appeal to men individually, and to all mankind. That is our legacy, our burden, and our joy.

14. Madison, *Notes of Debates*, p. 271.
15. Ibid., p. 272.

The Problem of the Household in the Second Spanish Period

THEODORE G. CORBETT

STUDY of the family is an endeavor which historians have normally left to the case analysis of anthropologists or to the charts of genealogists, but recently such work has become the preserve of social historians, who have adopted techniques from these disciplines.[1] A major thrust of the new investigations has been to deemphasize the family as an entity bound together by ties of kinship and to replace this conception with an idea of the family as the center of a functioning household. The collecting, counting, and formulation of family households, therefore, has become an important means of re-creating a community's social past.

Our Anglo-Saxon culture and contemporary environment have led us to think of the family and the household as almost synonymous: a household existing for each individual family. As might be expected, this condition was scarcely dominant in Florida's Second Spanish Period when a majority of households were crowded not only with immediate kin, but distant cousins, lodgers, slaves, servants, apprentices, and orphans. Certain households, furthermore, like the plantation, the *hacienda*, the manor, or the factory were organized solely for the purpose of profit. It is impossible, then, to think of the bulk of the households in the period from 1784 to 1821 as consisting of a single family. Instead, a household can be defined

1. Peter Laslett and Richard Wall, eds., *Household and Family in Past Time* (Cambridge, England, 1974); Robert Wells, *The Population of the British Colonies in America before 1776* (Princeton, New Jersey, 1975), pp. 297–333; Edward Shorter, *The Making of the Modern Family* (New York, 1975), pp. 22–53.

as having three characteristics: a common premises (most usually thought of as a roof over one's head), a division of labor in the task of managing the premises, and, least consistently, the traditional bonds of kinship.[2] This definition has the advantage of allowing us to ask questions not only about birth and marriage, but also about matters like privacy and racial relations or, even more important, about the degree to which the family household functioned as an economic unit.

In the Second Spanish Period, Florida's inhabitants were trying to build a new society that had twice been radically altered by evacuations: the Spanish in 1763–64 and the British in 1784–85. The change of regimes had left Floridians divided in terms of citizenship, ethnic background, and cultural attitude. Some residents traced their ancestors back to the First Spanish Period and consequently were designated natives, or *Floridanos*. Others were holdovers from the British Period and their tastes were similar to the British Americans who had settled in the Carolinas and Georgia. Still others were essentially European peasants, possessing Mediterranean cultural values that had been carried to America from Minorca, Greece, Italy, Corsica, Catalonia, and the Canary Islands. Finally there were the blacks, some of them victims of the African slave trade, but at this late date the majority were probably native Americans. Such a diversity of backgrounds made it inevitable that household structure would vary.

Two basic types of household structure were inherited from the British Period. One of these was the plantation, a form which the British introduced to Florida. The peculiar affinity of British Americans for the plantation was demonstrated by the failure of their philanthropic efforts to create permanent settlements of yeoman farmers at Rollestown in British Florida and in the early phases of Georgia's colonization.[3] British occupation of Florida proved far more successful and lucrative when plantations were established along the St. Marys and St. Johns rivers. Among them, Governor James Grant's villa, Lieutenant Governor John Moultrie's Bella

2. Laslett, "Introduction," in Laslett and Wall, *Household and Family*, pp. 24–25, 34–40.
3. Carita Doggett Corse, "Denys Rolle of Rollestown, A Pioneer for Utopia," *Florida Historical Quarterly* 7 (October 1928):115–34; on Georgia's development see Lawrence Henry Gipson, *The British Isles and the American Colonies: The Southern Plantations 1748–1754*, vol. 2, *The British Empire before the American Revolution* (New York, 1960), pp. 173–79.

The Household in the Second Spanish Period / 51

Vista and Rosetta Place, Richard Oswald's Mount Oswald, and Francis Philip Fatio's New Switzerland bear witness to the creation of a society of great planters.[4]

Besides the presence of these plantations, certain characteristics of a plantation society appeared in British Florida. In contrast to the First Spanish Period a high percentage of the population was black and the colony was less centered around St. Augustine. At the time of the Spanish evacuation in 1763, blacks and mulattoes numbered only one out of every ten East Floridians; by 1782, however, Governor Tonyn reported that they numbered three out of every four permanent inhabitants.[5] Whereas at the beginning of the eighteenth century the Spaniards had abandoned most of Florida's interior to concentrate around the fortifications of St. Augustine, only about half of East Florida's population resided there under the British.[6] Planters and entrepreneurs developed the land northward to Amelia Island and southward to New Smyrna.[7] British Florida had, moreover, another feature of plantation society: it exported crops to distant markets. In 1776, 65,000 oranges, 860 barrels of rice, and 58,295 pounds of indigo were sent to England and to the British American colonies.[8] Overall, the British province seemed to be following the path of neighboring South Carolina.

The structure of plantation households in British Florida is a matter of conjecture since censuses do not report them in detail. The material that does exist, such as the loyalist claims, must be treated with reserve for in many cases the claimants actually underestimated the value of their property.[9] Data for South Carolina and the British West Indies are much more complete and can provide clues to the identification of a plantation household. To begin with, it seems definite that the majority of inhabitants within a

4. Charles Mowat, *East Florida as a British Province, 1763–1784* (Gainesville, 1964), pp. 68–70.
5. Ibid., p. 126; Archivo General de Indias, Seville, Spain, *estante* 86, *cajón* 6, *legajo* 6/43, April 16, 1764, photostat in Stetson Collection, P. K. Yonge Library of Florida History, University of Florida, Gainesville.
6. John Jay TePaske, *The Governorship of Spanish Florida, 1700–1763* (Durham, N.C., 1961), pp. 110–16.
7. J. Leitch Wright, *Florida in the American Revolution* (Gainesville, 1975), pp. 4–7.
8. Mowat, *East Florida*, pp. 77–78; Helen Hornbeck Tanner, *Zéspedes in East Florida, 1784–1790* (Coral Gables, 1963), p. 140.
9. Eugene Fingerhut, "Uses and Abuses of the American Loyalists' Claims," *William and Mary Quarterly*, 3d. ser. 25 (April 1968):245–58.

plantation society were not great planters. Capitalists with thirty slaves or more were always a minority, the bulk of the white population consisting of small-scale farmers or of craftsmen with few or no slaves. It should thus come as no surprise that in 1771 only one-third of East Florida's male population was designated as planter or that in the 1784 evacuation census, laborers and carpenters outnumbered planters.[10]

But a certain household structure can be ascertained from examples of plantation societies in eighteenth-century South Carolina and the British West Indies. There households were more extensive than anywhere in British America, the mean size ranging from 9.5 members in South Carolina to 43.6 in Tobago.[11] Such figures were high not because of the size of the average family, but rather because of the scores of slaves that often worked for a lone white overseer. In these colonies neither black nor white families flourished, the number of surviving offspring being small, while the growth of the colony was dependant upon immigration. In the case of blacks this condition was not only a result of the rigors of their labor, but also was caused by the planter's preference for males in their prime years as field hands, leaving most plantations with fewer females than males. White families also tended to be small because many planters came as bachelors or left their families in their homeland, returning to domestic life after they had made their fortunes.[12] In South Carolina, though white families were not always limited in size, they rarely had a chance to increase because of high mortality caused by the prevalence of malaria in the rice fields.[13] In sum, plantation households were identified by thirty or more slaves as a labor force, directed by a white family of only a few members.

The second form of household that existed in the British Period was the peasant type, a form markedly in contrast with the plantation. It was found among Turnbull's bondsmen at New Smyrna, but did not flourish until 1777 when the majority of the Minorcans

10. Mowat, *East Florida*, p. 64; Library of Congress, East Florida Papers (hereafter cited as LC, EFP), B. 323A, Census Returns, 1784–1814, Census of October 20, 1784.
11. Wells, *The Population of the Colonies*, p. 300.
12. Richard Dunn, *Sugar and Slaves* (New York, 1972), pp. 94–97; Philip J. Greven, "The Average Size of Families and Households in the Province of Massachusetts in 1764 and in the United States in 1790: an Overview," in Laslett and Wall, *Household and Family*, pp. 557–59.
13. Peter Wood, *Black Majority: Negros in Colonial South Carolina from 1670 through the Stono Rebellion* (New York, 1974), pp. 63–91, 131–66.

The Household in the Second Spanish Period / 53

escaped to make homes in St. Augustine.[14] Established in the town, their households consisted of the conjugal domestic unit—the father, mother, and immediate children. Slaves, cousins, and servants were rare additions because the family could not afford to feed the extra mouths. Families were thus similar in size to the four or five members that are common today, not due to birth control but because of the high mortality rate. Before their arrival in St. Augustine the Minorcans had suffered a demographic disaster: in 1768 when they left Gibraltar they numbered 1,403; after their voyage to Florida the number was reduced to 1,225; when counted in January 1778 as new citizens of St. Augustine there were only 419.[15] This adversity had the effect of creating many conjugal units from the remarriage of widows and widowers who already had established families. Occasionally, more extensive households existed, usually among craftsmen who took apprentices and journeymen onto the premises to help with their trade. These Mediterranean folk also maintained an affinity for congregating in urban communities, even when engaged in farming, for they would leave their townhouses each day and go out to work in the fields.[16] Basically, these peasant households were made up of the classic nuclear family of Europe, where the conjugal unit served as the labor force, the town was the home, and only a minority could afford the luxury of slaves and servants.

What role did these two forms of household play in the Second Spanish Period? Certain population characteristics support the contention that the plantation household was as influential under the Spanish as it had been under the British. The dispersed pattern of the population remained, to the extent that in the censuses of 1785 and 1793 one-quarter of the population resided outside of St. Augustine, and in the census of 1815 the number grew to almost one-half.[17] This latter count actually showed that Amelia Island with

14. On the Minorcans see: E. P. Panagopoulos, *New Smyrna: An Eighteenth Century Greek Odyssey* (Gainesville, 1966); Jane Quinn, *Minorcans in Florida* (St. Augustine, 1975); Carita Doggett Corse, *Dr. Andrew Turnbull and the New Smyrna Colony of Florida* (Jacksonville, 1919).
15. Panagopoulos, *New Smyrna*, pp. 48, 54, 173–74.
16. Julian Pitt-Rivers, *The People of the Sierra* (Chicago and London, 1963), p. 42. Although not agreeing with his conception of peasant society as being limited to non-Europeans, Richard Morse's "Some Characteristics of Latin American Urban Society," *American Historical Review* 67 (January 1962):317–38, affirms the urban nature of Spanish colonization.
17. LC, EFP, B. 323A, Census Returns, 1784–1814, Census of 1785, Census of 1793, Census of 1815 (the last census is dated 1815 despite the Library of

1,481 persons had a larger civilian population than the capital city.[18] The percentage of blacks and mulattoes among the province's inhabitants also remained high, rather than reverting to the pattern of the First Spanish Period. Though the colored segment of society was never as extensive as it was in the estimate of 1782, it included one out of three persons in St. Augustine.[19] The 1815 census revealed a further rise so that 40 percent of the city's population was colored.[20] Though figures are more sketchy for rural areas, those of 1787 show that outside of the city, three out of five inhabitants were blacks or mulattoes.[21] Thus in the Second Spanish Period the population dispersed into rural areas and the colored population increased, conditions which were similar to those of the British Period.

At this point detailed analysis of household structure becomes necessary in order to determine which types of households were most numerous. A census of 1786, done for St. Augustine and the area within a fifteen mile radius, is most useful because it groups the inhabitants into 167 households.[22] Gathered by the Irish priest Thomas Hassett, the census includes most of the population, except the garrison and its dependents as well as a handful of officials employed by the royal treasury.[23] The list divides the inhabitants into four categories: Foreigners, Floridians, Minorcans (including Greeks, Italians, and Corsicans), and Spaniards. This is, therefore, one of the few documents allowing for analysis of the household in terms of ethnic and cultural groups. It will be recalled that the Foreigners were essentially British or British-Americans, holdovers

---

Congress citation); John Dunkle, "Population Change as an Element in the Historical Geography of St. Augustine," *Florida Historical Quarterly* 37 (July 1958):14–17, 20.

18. Census of 1815; Dunkle, "Population Change," p. 20. Dunkle's figure for Amelia Island is mistakenly recorded as 1,491.

19. Census of 1785, Census of 1793; Dunkle, "Population Change," p. 21.

20. Census of 1815; Dunkle, "Population Change," pp. 20–21.

21. Tanner, *Zéspedes*, pp. 127–36.

22. LC, EFP, B. 323A, Census Returns, 1784–1814, Census of Father Thomas Hassett, 1786. A portion of this census has been reproduced by Joseph Byrne Lockey as "The St. Augustine Census of 1786," *Florida Historical Quarterly* 18 (July 1939):11–31.

23. Unlike enumerations in the First Spanish Period, those of the Second Spanish Period normally include only the civilian population. As a result, to gain an idea of overall population one would have to add the garrison, treasury officials, and their dependents to the censuses of civilian population. The number of noncivilians can be estimated as 1,500 to 2,000.

from the previous regime. The Floridians were those people who had been born in St. Augustine during the First Spanish Period and who now returned with their families. The Minorcans were, of course, the remains of Turnbull's colony. The last of these settlers were peninsulars, Spaniards who had migrated from the Old World, in this case particularly from the Canary Islands and Catalonia. The census did not treat blacks and mulattoes separately, probably because few of them headed households.

Before putting this census to a test, some familiarity must be established with different types of households.[24] It would be naïve to expect the households of this census to fall neatly into place as being either of the plantation or the peasant forms. The document shows, in fact, at least six distinct types. First and most obvious is the household made up of a single individual, the solitary. Then there is a second type where no kinship existed between the head of the household and its other members. Such a "no kin" form was typical of the plantation where a single bachelor oversaw scores of slaves. Another category that has impressed scholars as dominant in much of seventeenth- and eighteenth-century Europe is the nuclear, or simple, household, consisting of the conjugal family unit: father, mother, and children. This classical form has already been noted as prevalent among peasants like the Minorcans. If this nuclear household added servants, slaves, or relatives, it became an nuclear extended household, a common occurrence among a sizeable minority of the population. Two more complicated varieties of extended family households have also been recognized: the stem and the multiple types. The former is identified by the existence of the conjugal unit plus grandparents, in other words, a junior and a senior couple. Such a form represents a stage in household development where grandparents relinquish leadership over a premises and retire, passing their duties on to their children. The latter consists of two families that live in the same dwelling and share the duties of operating it. Though kinship between the two families was not necessary, this form was often headed by brothers or by a brother and a sister, who banded together because neither family could run the household singly. To see the household in its full complexity, our

---

24. Although I take full responsibility for this classification of household types, the categories are based on Laslett and Wall, *Household and Family,* pp. 28–32 and on Shorter, *Modern Family,* pp. 29–39.

TABLE 1
Types of Households in the 1786 Census (%)

Group	Solitary	No Kin	Nuclear	Extended Stem	Multiple	Total Households
Foreigners		21.7	47.8	4.3	13.0	23
Floridians	7.1	35.7	21.4	7.1	14.3	14
Spaniards	25.0	18.8	25.0			16
Minorcans	4.4	7.0	29.8	1.8	1.8	114
Total	6.0	12.6	31.1	2.4	4.2	167

The Household in the Second Spanish Period / 57

study must be broadened to six types: solitary, "no kin," nuclear, nuclear extended, stem, and multiple.

The results of counting the different types of households found in the four census groups can be seen in Table 1. Clearly predominant among Foreigners were the extended nuclear and "no kin" forms. The same is true of the Floridians, though the strength of the two types is reversed. Since both these forms of household require additional members beyond the conjugal unit, it is in these two groups that plantations were most likely to be present. Meanwhile, the Spaniards and Minorcans seem to belong to a different tradition. Among them the simple nuclear type appears most often, while the

TABLE 2
TYPES OF NUCLEAR HOUSEHOLDS IN THE 1786 CENSUS (%)

Group	Simple	Multiple	Extended Simple	Multiple	Total Households
Foreigners	20.0	6.7	73.3		15
Floridians	20.0	20.0	60.0		5
Spaniards	55.5	11.1	33.3		9
Minorcans	52.0	14.6	18.8	14.6	96
Total	47.2	13.6	28.0	11.2	125

nuclear extended form holds second place. The Spaniards were exceptional because they had a considerable number of solitary and "no kin" households, reflecting the fact that many had not formed families because they had recently arrived from the Iberian Peninsula. Stem and multiple families appear to be rare in the population as a whole, though Foreigners and Floridians were most likely to have some. Overall, the dominating number of Minorcan households makes their nuclear and nuclear extended pattern the most characteristic of the community.

It would be misleading to think of the nuclear households of the census as being identical with those of today. Table 2 takes both the nuclear and nuclear extended households and shows that a number of them were multiple in the sense that they had been formed from previously separate families.[25] Such unions were usu-

25. In Table 2 the term "simple" is used to describe a nuclear household formed from a single family by a single marriage, while the term "multiple" describes a nuclear household formed by two or more families from two or more marriages. In this instance the term "multiple" should not be confused with the extended multiple household in Table 1.

TABLE 3
Household Size in the 1786 Census

Number of Members	1	2	3	4	5	6	7	8	9	10	11	13	14	16	17	20	51	63
Foreigners (23 households)																		
Number of households		2	5	3	3			1	1			1	1	1	2	1	1	1
Percent of households		9	22	13	13			4	4			4	4	4	9	4	4	7
Floridians (14 households)																		
Number of households	1	1	2	2	4				1	1			1					1
Percent of households	7	7	14	14	29				7	7			7					7
Spaniards (16 households)																		
Number of households	4	1	1	4	3	2	1											
Percent of households	25	6	6	25	19	13	6											
Minorcans (114 households)																		
Number of households	5	16	17	21	15	16	12	2	5	2	1	2						
Percent of households	4	14	15	18	13	14	11	2	4	2	1	2						

ally between a widow and a widower. Though the majority of Foreign nuclear families were similar to those of the twentieth century, in other words headed by a couple from a single marriage, three out of ten Minorcan nuclear families, and two out of ten Florida nuclear families were created from a second or a third marriage. One out of every four nuclear families in the community was created in this way. The prevalence of such households, particularly among the Minorcans and Floridians, fortifies the contention that these groups had suffered from high mortality rates in the years before the census.

The information in these two tables lacks, however, an important dimension: size. Without some idea of it, no differentiation could be made, for instance, between a full-fledged plantation and a nuclear extended family with a few slaves. Table 3 presents household size to complement the previous tables. These figures suggest that Foreigners and Floridians on one hand and Spaniards and Minorcans on the other followed similar household patterns. In the former two groups, households of three to five members were most common; but there was a considerable number of them that were larger: one out of four among the Foreigners had thirteen or more members, one out of five among the Floridians had ten or more members. The average family in the latter group was a bit more extensive, consisting among Spaniards of from four to six members and among Minorcans of from two to seven members. But while the families were slightly larger, there were few extensive households. No Spanish households had more than seven members, and the numerous Minorcans were limited to one with eleven and two with thirteen members. Thus, the Foreigners' and Floridians' households contained more people than those of any other group.

If the components of these households are examined in terms of the number of children, slaves, and free coloreds, then an idea of the economic structure can be obtained. It is plain from Table 4, which deals with children, that Minorcan women bore them more consistently and in greater profusion, from two to four in each household, than any other group. Spaniards and Floridians were least likely to have offspring, though even among them, over half the households had children, usually in numbers of one to three. The pattern of residence for children among the Foreigners ranged between these two extremes. Table 5 shows that whereas Minorcan households had the most children, they were least likely to have slaves. Three-quarters of the Minorcan and Spanish households had no slaves, while only half of those of the Foreigners and Floridians were without them. These latter groups had the most slaves, a quarter of the Foreign households having six or more, while one Floridian household topped all others with fifty-three. Table 6 demonstrates that the number of free coloreds in the population was minimal, but that they were also most likely to be found among the Floridians. In sum, these tables show that many Foreign and Floridian households were dependent upon slave and free colored labor, while those of the Minorcans were sustained by their own children,

TABLE 4
CHILDREN PER HOUSEHOLD IN THE 1786 CENSUS

Number of Children	0	1	2	3	4	5	6	14
Foreigners								
Number of households	7	8	5	1	1		1	
Percent of households	30	35	22	4	4		4	
Percent of children		26	32	10	13		19	
Floridians								
Number of households	6	3	1	2		1		1
Percent of households	43	21	7	14		7		7
Percent of children		10	7	20		17		47
Spaniards								
Number of households	7	4	3	2				
Percent of households	44	25	19	13				
Percent of children		25	38	38				
Minorcans								
Number of households	25	20	30	18	16	2	3	
Percent of households	22	18	26	16	14	2	3	
Percent of children		9	27	24	28	4	8	

and those of the Spanish were apparently deficient in both slaves and children. The tables indicate that Foreigners and Floridians were most likely to have plantation households, while Minorcans and Spaniards clung to the peasant norms of the Old World.

Lest use of these tables create a healthy skepticism that the flesh and blood reality of family life has been turned into mere figures, discussion of specific households is required. On this level the intricacies of unique family situations can be dealt with. A dozen families have been chosen for analysis and each one will be presented with the aid of an ideograph.

Among Foreign households, that of Jamie McGirt can be identi-

TABLE 5

SLAVES PER HOUSEHOLD IN THE 1786 CENSUS

Number of Slaves	0	1	2	3	4	5	6	9	10	11	14	15	46	53
Foreigners														
Number of households	11	2	2				2		1	2	1	1	1	1
Percent of households	48	9	9				9		4	9	4	4	4	7
Percent of slaves		1	3				9		8	17	11	12	36	78
Floridians														
Number of households	7	3	1		1		1							
Percent of households	50	21	7		7		7							
Percent of slaves		4	3		6		9							
Spaniards														
Number of households	12	1	2			1								
Percent of households	75	6	13			6								
Percent of slaves		10	40			50								
Minorcans														
Number of households	86	14	3	7	3			1						
Percent of households	75	12	3	6	3			1						
Percent of slaves		23	10	34	19			15						

fied in Figure 1 as one of nuclear extended form. The brother of the famous renegade, McGirt was a Lutheran from Carolina whose reputation and livelihood were clouded by dishonor because of his support of his brother.[26] By occupation McGirt was a farmer, who in the 1790s held eight hundred acres on three different farms. He appears to have cultivated each farm to exhaustion and then moved on to the next. Eventually, he obtained a grant of forest and was able to follow the more profitable endeavor of providing lumber for

TABLE 6
COLORED FREEMEN PER HOUSEHOLD IN THE 1786 CENSUS

Number of Freemen	1	2	3	7	9
Foreigners	1		1		
Floridians	3	1			1
Minorcans	2			1	

houses and fences. In the census, his larger than average household consisted of fourteen members, including him, his wife, five sons, a daughter, and four male and two female slaves. Ranging from twelve to twenty years of age, the sons were all unmarried and formed the family's principal labor force. McGirt's extensive number of children was unusual among the Foreigners, his household being more typical of the farmers of the Carolina Piedmont.

Other nuclear extended households among the Foreigners were more dependent upon slave labor. McGirt was classified in the census as a mere farmer, while Doña Honoria Clark was distinguished as a planter. This Irish widow (Fig. 2) with only her sixteen-year-old daughter and fourteen-year-old son depended upon her fifteen slaves to bear the burden of the household duties. Besides being a planter, she ran a store and had a twenty-six-year-old Irish gentleman as a lodger, as well as a young Spanish orphan, who no doubt helped with chores. Though her conjugal family was smaller than McGirt's, her household was much more substantial, and her involvement in several enterprises made her something of an entrepreneur.

26. Joseph B. Lockey, *East Florida 1783–1785* (Berkeley and Los Angeles, 1949), pp. 21, 246, 338–54, 525–31; Historical Records Survey (hereafter cited as HRS), *Spanish Land Grants in Florida*, 5 vols. (Tallahassee, 1940–41), 1:219–21, 3:122, 4:95–97.

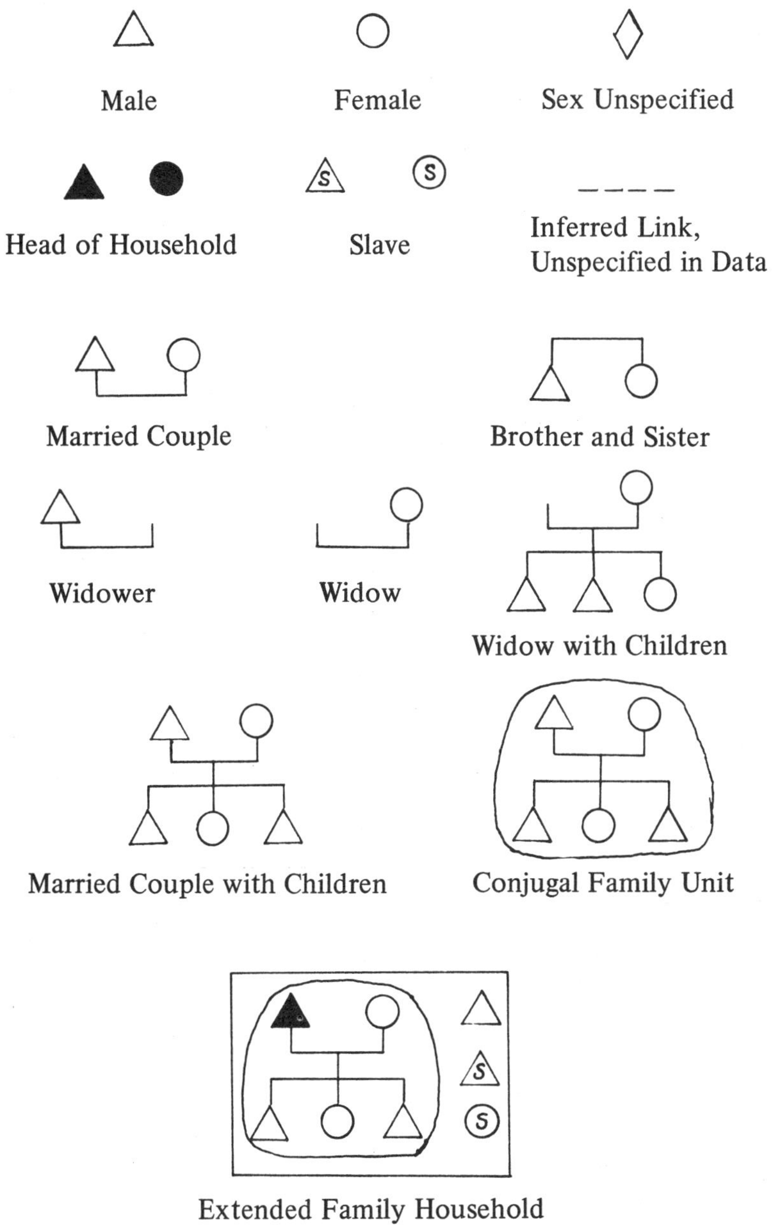

△ ○ ◇
Male   Female   Sex Unspecified

▲ ●   ⟨s⟩ Ⓢ   - - - -
Head of Household   Slave   Inferred Link, Unspecified in Data

Married Couple   Brother and Sister

Widower   Widow

Widow with Children

Married Couple with Children   Conjugal Family Unit

Extended Family Household

Key to Ideographs

Ideographs representing household structure:
St. Augustine, 1786

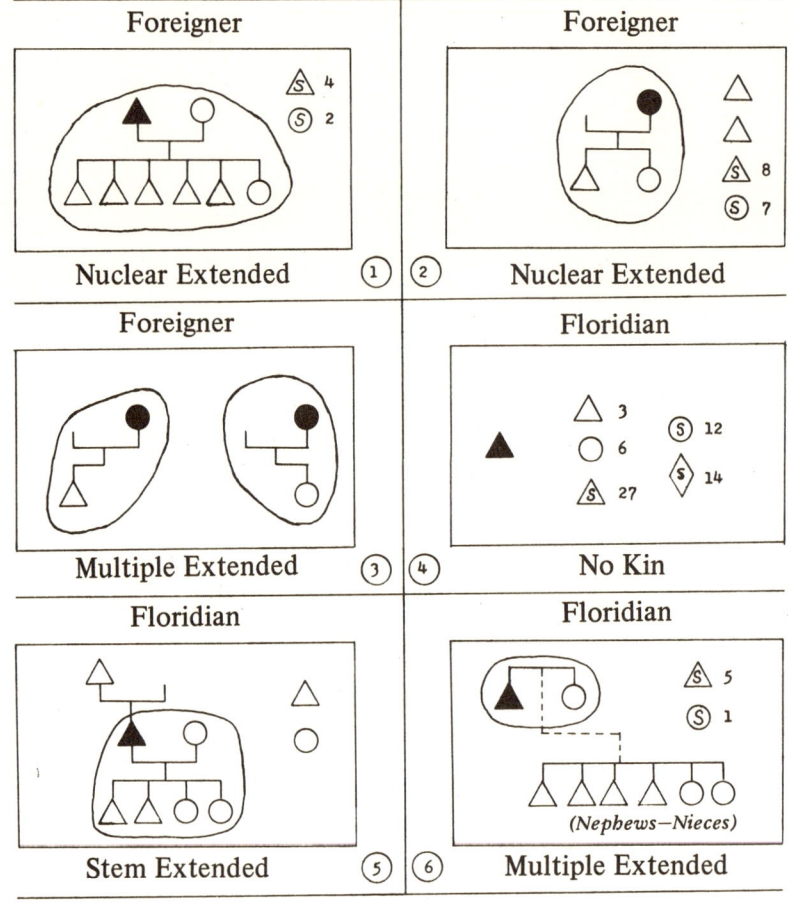

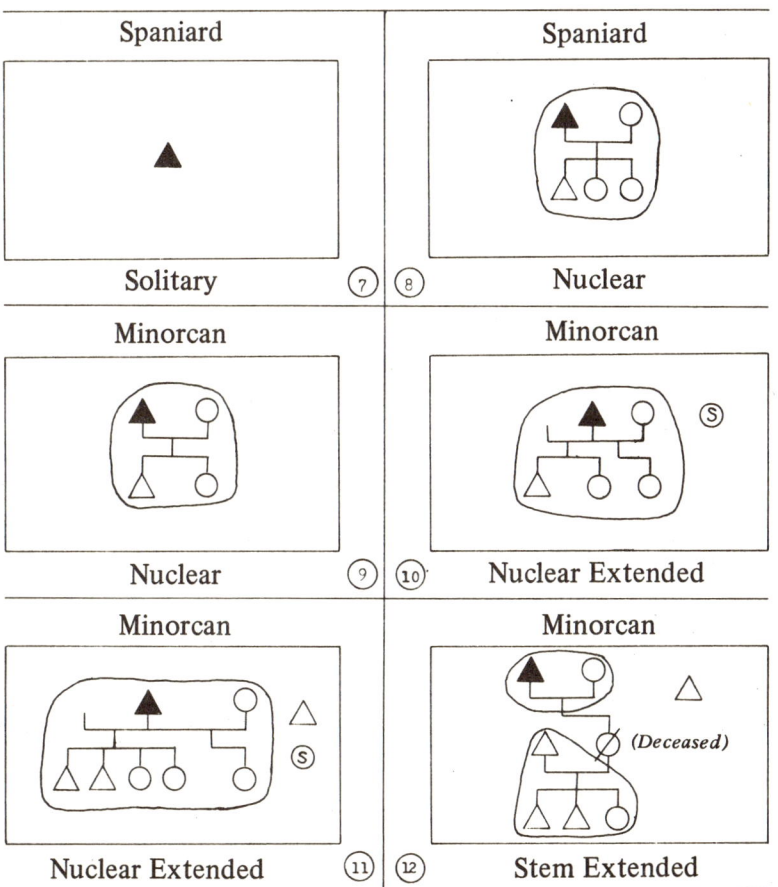

Most Foreign households were smaller than these two examples, that of Maria Collen and Maria Luisa Rodriguez being closer to the norm. Only four people are found in their dwelling (Fig. 3), and none were slaves. This household was multiple because of the two families who shared it. Maria Collen's husband did not live on the premises and Maria Luisa was a widow; each woman had a single child. There were no kinship ties between the two families and the two women were actually of different faiths: Maria Collen was Protestant, Maria Luisa was Catholic. Here was a type of extended household which was smaller than many conjugal families or nuclear households. Most likely it was created because neither woman wished to face the difficulties of running a separate household.

The most extensive household in the entire census belonged to a Floridian, Francisco Xavier Sanchez. His classification as a native was based upon his birth in St. Augustine in 1736, the son of José Sanchez de Ortigosa from Ronda, Spain, but uniquely he had stayed in Florida under the British regime, an experience which left him with strong ties to the Foreigners.[27] Figure 4, derived from the census, presents him as a bachelor, forty years old (he was actually fifty), without any kin, the master of fifty-three slaves (twenty-seven male, twelve female, and fourteen children) and nine free mulattoes. The location of this household is unclear since Sanchez owned several houses in St. Augustine, while his principal estate was located on the San Diego Plains, eighteen miles north of the city. Worked by slaves, his lands produced beef for consumption by the garrison of Castillo de San Marcos. He was a self-made man, who in the words of Governor Tonyn "rose from a state of obscure poverty to a degree of affluence seldom attained."[28] Sanchez also had more of a family than is apparent from the census. His black mistress bore him eight children but this relationship ended in 1787, when he married Theophilus Hill's young daughter. Here was a man who managed a household which appeared to be a classical plantation.

Sanchez' household was exceptional, and equally exceptional were the few stem and multiple households that appeared among the Floridians. As an example of the stem form there is the household

27. The record of Sanchez' birth is found in the Cathedral Records, St. Augustine Parish, photostatic copies in the St. Augustine Historical Society, St. Augustine, Florida; Tanner, *Zéspedes*, p. 125.
28. Lockey, *East Florida*, p. 215.

headed by Don Francisco Huet, which contained not only his wife and immediate children but his seventy-eight-year-old father. Figure 5 shows that Huet included the older generation in his household, probably out of respect for his father, as well as his ability to provide for him. Besides this stem family household, there were also multiple family households, like that of Sebastian and Josepha Espinosa. As diagrammed in Figure 6, this brother and sister accepted the responsibility of raising their nieces and nephews, so that the household was a composite of three separate families. Such a pattern was testimony to the high mortality that this family had suffered in Cuba.

The peninsulars had arrived from Europe the same year as the census and hence their households had been least exposed to the American environment. One-quarter of them were of the solitary structure, such as that of Antonio Rivera (Fig. 7). A sailor and native of Catalonia, he ran a wine shop in competition with other Spanish bachelors, although two years after the census he was an intern in the Royal Hospital of San Ambrasio.[29] He was at a marriageable age, thirty-two, but he was evidently too impoverished to take on that responsibility. Another peninsular household, that of Joseph Antonio Coruña, a native of the Canary Islands, is recorded in Figure 8. He brought his wife, sixteen-year-old son, and nine- and six-year-old daughters to manage a farm in the New World. Nuclear households of Coruña's type were most popular among the Spaniards, showing that it was more common for families to be transferred intact from Europe to America.

The Minorcan community had existed in Florida for eighteen years, yet their household structure remained almost as European as those of the newly arrived Spaniards. Seen in Figure 9, the household of Juan Joaneda, for instance, was also nuclear. Born in Minorca, Joaneda had lived in New Smyrna before the exodus of 1777.[30] In St. Augustine he married Magdalena Marin, the daughter of a cobbler, and the census shows him with a young daughter and a younger son. Although identified in the census as a mere laborer, he prospered, building a townhouse, cultivating a farm between the North River and Guana Creek, and eventually marrying his eldest daughter to the eligible Floridian Nicolas Sanchez. This success was marred, however, by the death of his wife in the early 1790s,

29. HRS, 3:147–50.
30. Ibid., 1:41, 3:195, 5:43–45.

and his house was sold after 1807. Joaneda's household was clearly that of a young Minorcan family, prepared to experience the fortunes of life in St. Augustine.

As mentioned, one-third of the Minorcan nuclear and nuclear extended families were multiple or made up of previously separate families. This is the background for the household in Figure 10. It is that of Francisco Pellicer, a carpenter from Minorca, who had previously settled in New Smyrna and married Margarita Femanías.[31] Though five children were born to the couple in Turnbull's colony, only the eldest, a son, and a daughter survived to appear on the census. Five years before the census was taken, Margarita died, and in 1783, Pellicer was remarried to Juana Vila Ferrer. This union produced a daughter, Maria, who appears on the census. By 1780, Pellicer lived in his own attached house in the town, but seven years later he sold this house and moved to a farm along the Matanzas River. In his later years he evidently prospered, fathering more children, acquiring three or four slaves, and in 1798 building a townhouse from which he traveled back and forth to his extensive rural acreage. Here was a household which recovered from the demographic disasters of New Smyrna and went on to prosper in St. Augustine.

The structure of households headed by people from the other Mediterranean areas varied little from the pattern of the Minorcans. The nuclear extended family of an Italian, Rocco Leonardi, is diagrammed in Figure 11. Though evidently prolific, his family did not escape the high mortality rate that plagued the Minorcans. He was married to Esperanza Bolla at New Smyrna, and they had two children before she died in 1774.[32] His remarriage to a Minorcan widow, Agueda Coll, was more lasting, and in the years that followed, they had eleven children. The census records show his household with four of these eleven children, as well as Agueda's son by a previous marriage, and two blacks, one free and one a slave. Though a mere laborer, Leonardi prospered, as is indicated by the fact that one year after the census he owned four houses, fifty acres of land, and two horses. This success was apparently based on his abilities as a wine merchant and grape grower. In the 1790s he became a full-fledged farmer cultivating two thousand acres on the North River,

31. Overton Ganong, "The Peso De Burgo–Pellicer Houses," *El Escribano* 12 (July 1975):82; Quinn, *Minorcans*, pp. 152–63.
32. HRS, 4:48–52, 5:9–11.

only fifteen miles from St. Augustine, developing a reputation for the best fruit and wine in the area. Once again the census shows a household prospering after the hard times at New Smyrna.

The households of Minorcan craftsmen were often somewhat more extensive than the norm, and that of Francisco Marin, a shoemaker (Fig. 12), is an example. The head of this stem family household had learned his trade in his native Catalonia. Evidently he had migrated from there to Minorca and married a native of the island, Magdalena Escodero.[33] They had come to New Smyrna and had several children, of whom only a son, Francisco, and two daughters, Tecla and the previously mentioned Magdalena, survived to marry. Tecla's spouse was a Corsican, Elias Medici, whose family had originally come from Italy. She died before 1786, leaving Elias to take care of their three children and to carry on his work as a cobbler. He and the children came to live with his father-in-law because the census showed them as part of the household. Another member of Marin's establishment was a journeyman carpenter, Antonio Llambias, whose story was one of courage in the face of adversity: his entire family was wiped out in only a few years. A Minorcan, he arrived in St. Augustine in 1777 with his father, after his mother, two sisters, and two brothers had died at New Smyrna. His father succumbed within a year, and Antonio was orphaned at the age of sixteen. Without money or security he was forced to apprentice himself to the master carpenter Martin Hernandez. Perhaps there was some sort of exchange between Hernandez' and Marin's households, a situation which the census supports, for Marin's fifteen-year-old son, Francisco, was an apprentice in the master carpenter's household. In 1789, Llambias left Marin's household to marry, while Francisco, by 1793, had returned to be a part of his father's home. The Medici children continued to live with their grandparents, even after 1793 when their father was no longer present. In the 1790s, Marin built a stone house to accommodate his still numerous family. Thus the Marin household was maintained by several generations of the family, as well as a bachelor craftsman, rather than depending upon the presence of slaves. Here is an indication that this household maintained the traditions of the Old World longer than others.

Having thoroughly examined the census, I can make some overall

33. Doris Wiles, "The Fernandez-Llambias House," *El Escribano* 4 (April 1967):6; Panagopoulos, *New Smyrna*, pp. 61, 62, 181, 183; Quinn, *Minorcans*, p. 233.

70 / Eighteenth-Century Florida and the Revolution

observations. The nuclear household was unquestionably the most common type, although few existed among Foreigners and Floridians who were not a majority in the census. Two out of five households were nuclear, and among the Minorcans it was the dominant type. As pointed out, these nuclear households were neither as prevalent nor created from a single marriage as often as they are today, but their abundant presence in the census indicates that the nuclear household was, as some historians have previously asserted,[34] the most popular form in Western preindustrial society. If, in fact, the nuclear extended households are added to those of the simple nuclear type, as has been done also, then three-fourths of the households belong to these two forms.[35] The Florida community, having an average of only 5.7 persons per premises, did not produce households with as many members as the plantation societies of South Carolina or of the British West Indies.

Before concluding that East Florida could not have maintained a plantation society in view of its many nuclear families, it is important to see if there is another side to this question. The evidence of substantial plantation development is, to say the least, weak, with only two full-scale plantations, three more modest establishments with planters as heads of household, and the households of two farmers that might qualify. Fifteen households were extensive enough to have ten or more members: seven of them headed by Foreigners, five by Minorcans, three by Floridians, and none by Spaniards. Of these, five were headed by merchants or tradesmen, one by a craftman, one by a sailor, and one by the sacristan; so these can be eliminated. Of interest as plantation households were the five headed by planters and two headed by farmers. The names of these planters and farmers are well known to those familiar with the British Period since they were all Foreigners, save Sanchez, who was only technically a Floridian. The list included (besides Sanchez): the planters Francis Philip Fatio, Juan Hudson, Doña Honoria Clark, and Jesse Fish and the farmers Theophilus Hill and Jaime McGirt. Of the planters, three of the households were nuclear extended in structure and two were of "no kin" composition. The census showed the five planters with 149 slaves and 10 free blacks, 63 percent of all slaves recorded, or an average of 30 slaves per

34. Laslett, "Preface," p. xi, and "Introduction," pp. 8–10, 59–60, 72–73, in Laslett and Wall, *Household and Family*.
35. Laslett, "Introduction," ibid., pp. 29, 85.

The Household in the Second Spanish Period / 71

household. Actually only two households, those of Sanchez and Hudson, contributed two-thirds of all the slaves, designating their establishments as the only full-fledged plantations in the area. Here, then, is East Florida's modest planter aristocracy.

It cannot be denied that the 1786 census has definite limitations in settling the question of the degree to which these two societies flourished. Conclusions drawn from the census are limited to the vicinity of St. Augustine, while plantations were more numerous in the distant rural areas of East Florida. The 1786 census, for instance, showed Fatio's household, which consisted of sixteen members, of whom eleven were slaves, as smaller than that of Doña Honoria Clark. The bulk of Fatio's wealth was located, however, outside of St. Augustine on the St. Johns River at New Switzerland, which was worked by no fewer than seventy-nine slaves.[36] The census did not take into account plantations along the St. Johns or in the other areas of rural East Florida. The census, moreover, gives only a view of conditions at the beginning of the Second Spanish Period, and it must be assumed that there were changes over the next thirty-five years.

Such deficiencies can be remedied to an extent by placing the census in broader context, sketching household conditions in rural East Florida and briefly explaining what happened after 1786. One year after the census, for example, Father Michael O'Reilly accompanied Governor Zéspedes on an inspection of the province, keeping account of the households visited. Though more rudimentary than the 1786 census, this document does provide complementary information on rural East Florida.[37] It indicates that there were few slaves in the north between the St. Marys and the St. Johns rivers or on the Talbot Islands, but considerable numbers along the St. Johns where Fatio, Sanchez, Hill, and William Pengree had plantations. Taken as a whole, O'Reilly's figures showed more slaves living outside of St. Augustine than the 1786 census counted in the town and its suburbs. Later in the period there is evidence of a shift in plantation development from the St. Johns to the coastal islands between that river and the St. Marys. The most notorious of these planters was the British-American Zephaniah Kingsley, who in the 1800s moved from the St. Johns to establish his plantation on

36. Census of October 20, 1784.
37. Tanner, Zéspedes, pp. 127–36.

72 / Eighteenth-Century Florida and the Revolution

Fort George Island.[38] From this location, Kingsley participated in the slave trade, training African blacks in his fields and then selling them illegally in Georgia and South Carolina.

In the years after the 1787 visitation, however, the planters seem to have lost a good deal of their influence over East Florida. Their hold over the land seemed secure in 1785, when Fatio asserted that the Minorcans and Spaniards had congregated in the town as petty shopkeepers, artisans, and proprietors of liquor canteens rather than as cultivators of the soil.[39] Even the Floridians seemed to be no threat as they, he complained, were content to depend upon the Crown's subsidy for their livelihood. Fatio's appraisal of these rival ethnic groups was substantiated by Zéspedes' opinion that the newly arrived Canary Islanders showed no inclination for either industry or cultivation.[40] But while the Foreigners enjoyed these early years as the leading men of enterprise, in the 1790s the situations changed considerably. Following through on the promise of Zéspedes that the Crown would grant them land according to the number in each family,[41] the Minorcans began to move into rural East Florida. This settlement of the interior is exemplified by the previously mentioned households of Joaneda, Pellicer, and Leonardi. The scope of their efforts was limited to relatively small plots within easy access of St. Augustine, particularly along the North and Matanzas rivers, including the San Diego Plains toward the St. Johns River. Farms of this type were called *estancias*, or truck farms, common in Mediterranean Europe and in Cuba.[42] They were managed by nuclear families, supplemented by a few slaves, the households working together as a single unit. The produce of these farms was sold in St. Augustine and, as noted, residence on the land was often only daily or seasonal, the family retiring to spend the night or a portion of the year in a townhouse. Though the size of the estancia was small, when united these numerous farms were unquestionably a challenge to the great plantations.

While exploitation of the land increased, there is evidence that

38. Philip May, "Zephaniah Kingsley, Nonconformist (1765–1843)," *Florida Historical Quarterly* 23 (January 1945):145–59.
39. Lockey, *East Florida*, p. 481.
40. Tanner, *Zéspedes*, pp. 125, 139.
41. Lockley, *East Florida*, pp. 461–63.
42. The influence of the estancia in pre-nineteenth-century Cuba is discussed by Herbert Klein, *Slavery in the Americas: A Comparative Study of Virginia and Cuba* (Chicago, 1967), pp. 143–49.

cultivation, particularly of staple crops, decreased. Fatio himself no longer called for the production of rice or indigo, but hoped instead to develop a naval stores industry.[43] Sanchez' vast acreage was not organized as a classical plantation, but as a hacienda, similar to the extensive ranches of Mexico which provided meat and hides for local consumption. Ranching and the exploitation of the forest for lumber and naval stores appear to have been much more popular and profitable than tilling the soil. The transition from farming to these other endeavors was relatively easy. Sebastian Espinosa, for example, fenced five hundred unproductive acres on the San Diego Plains, placed stock on it, lived there for a while in a house, and soon had a modestly successful ranch.[44] Where grass or forest was not plentiful, one could follow the example of Miguel Chapuz, whose household at New Smyrna engaged in the management of a turtle farm, an enterprise which provided this delicacy for the cooks of St. Augustine.[45] Such evidence indicates that both planters and estancia farmers rivaled each other in the sale of meat and lumber in St. Augustine's markets.

The rise of ranching, lumbering, and, to a lesser extent, the estancias pointed out the difficulties of maintaining plantations and farms for cultivation. For one, the sandy soil would not hold seed and after only a year or two was exhausted. One Floridian, Lorenzo Rodríguez, had fenced, cultivated, and improved three hundred acres which he proudly dubbed Buena Vista; but it was reported that in the twelve years he occupied it he made little profit because of the sterility of the soil.[46] Such land required intense cultivation and fertilization, a form of farming which was only practical in the estancias within and about St. Augustine.

Besides the problem of the infertility of the soil there was also a danger of brigandage in rural areas. Indians and renegade bandits ravaged isolated plantations and farms. There is the case of the widow Nicolasa Gomez, who claimed to have built buildings and put six slaves to work on a land grant on the Hillsborough River, far from St. Augustine, but "Indians and rebels" interrupted her effort to develop the grant and on at least one occasion in the early 1800s, Indians drove her workers away.[47] Nor were the great plant-

43. Lockey, *East Florida*, pp. 479–80.
44. HRS, 3:50–51.
45. Ibid., 5:34–35.
46. Ibid., 4:250–52.
47. Ibid., 3:191–92.

74 / Eighteenth-Century Florida and the Revolution

ers immune from such hazards: during the raids of 1812, Fatio's plantation house at New Switzerland was destroyed by Indians.[48] These conditions made it wise to live and farm within the vicinity of St. Augustine rather than opening virgin land, an enterprise so necessary to the maintenance of a plantation.

The urbanization of a sizeable minority of East Florida's black population was also not conducive to a plantation society. Though planters held the bulk of slave labor in both St. Augustine and the rural areas, probably one-third of the blacks in East Florida worked on the estancias or were household servants. That the colored segment of St. Augustine's population prospered is indicated by the aforementioned rise in their numbers from 1786 to 1815. By this latter date, manumission and miscegenation had some effect, for 12 percent of the colored group was free, and one in seven of them was mulatto.[49] The presence of these pockets within the population no doubt reflects the urban environment where slave participation in household and family duties made manumission and miscegenation more likely than in rural areas.[50] One should not exaggerate the extent of this process, for Pensacola had a much more liberal attitude toward its colored population. Blacks there were often free artisans and tradesmen, while black women shared households as mistresses of white men.[51] St. Augustine was more segregated and conservative, probably as a result of attempts by Minorcans to monopolize crafts and compete with blacks as a source of labor. Unlike many Spanish-American communities, the Minorcans provided St. Augustine with a group of enterprising craftsmen and tradesmen. Still, St. Augustine offered blacks an urban alternative to the plantation, an alternative where some of them could gain their freedom and a degree of social status. Again, the prospects of maintaining a plantation society appear to have been bleak.

The present state of research on the household in this period prevents the assertion of hasty conclusions. One piece of evidence, the 1786 census, has been thoroughly analyzed, but there is a great deal

48. Susan L'Engle, "Notes of My Family and Recollections of My Early Life," manuscript in St. Augustine Historical Society, St. Augustine, Florida, p. 20. This is a typescript apparently taken from a book of the same title printed in New York at the Knickerbocker Press in 1888.
49. Census of 1815.
50. This statement was true under similar conditions in Cuba; see Klein, *Slavery*, pp. 62–65, 146–47.
51. Duvon Corbitt, "The Last Spanish Census of Pensacola, 1820," *Florida Historical Quarterly* 24 (July 1945):34–38.

The Household in the Second Spanish Period / 75

more to do. What has been achieved at this point is the establishment of a framework from which to approach the social and perhaps the economic history of the age. This interpretation of the period is based on two types of households and, more basically, on two distinct life-styles: the one cherished by the British-American planters who sought to continue the ways of the previous regime and perpetuate a plantation society much as existed in South Carolina; the other represented by the Minorcan nuclear households, where the traditions of Mediterranean peasants were maintained and enterprises centered upon the labor of the family. Both social segments had a part to play in Florida's Second Spanish Period, and tracing their development after 1786 will provide impetus for further research in this much neglected period. Here also is an interpretation which offers a new perspective for social history, based not upon the Marxist conception of class distinction and conflict, but rather upon ethnic and cultural contrast, particularly as found within the household structure. Let us make the best of this new learning.

Mitres and Flags:

Colonial Religion in the British and

Second Spanish Periods

MICHAEL V. GANNON

BY the time of the Treaty of Paris of 1763, Spanish Catholicism in Florida was in a greatly weakened condition when compared with its state of health in the previous hundred years. Following the catastrophic attacks on the Guale, Apalache, and Timucua Indian missions by the Englishman Colonel James Moore in the first decade of the eighteenth century, Spanish evangelization of aboriginal inhabitants of the peninsula and panhandle regions entered upon a long period of depression and decline. The Order of Friars Minor, or Franciscans, to whom the Indian *doctrinas* had been entrusted a century and a half before, lost everything: their villages, their zeal, their hope, and their influence. It is a tragic story best read in a more detailed history, but it needs to be said that their losses were brought upon themselves by themselves, as much as they were by Moore's marauders. Abandonment of the original Franciscan spirit, internal rivalries between Creoles and *Peninsulares,* and constant disputes with the secular clergy and governors must be recognized as the prime reasons for their ultimate collapse. By 1763, all management of Indians and mestizos had fallen through default into the hands of the secular clergy, and only ten Franciscans remained in Florida service, from a high of seventy in 1655 and from twenty-five in 1738. The mission era was over, and it would never be revived. The secular priests fared little better in the twilight years of Spain's first possession of Florida. Their work with the garrison and civilian list, and later with the Indians and mestizos, was similarly compromised by internal dissensions, conflicts with the friars, and clerical involvement in the soldiers' mutiny of 1758. Both preaching and the administration of sacraments had become pedestrian and uninspired. When on July 20, 1763, a regiment of English redcoats paraded through the plaza of St. Augustine, it brought an abrupt end to the hopes of the church after sixty years of obvious ecclesiastical deterioration. One year later no more than eight Roman Catholics, all laymen, could be found anywhere on the peninsula.[1]

In order to secure a financial return on the church properties in and around St. Augustine, the presidio's *cura* and Franciscan superior arranged for Don Juan Elixio de la Puente, royal auditor of the colony, to dispose of the properties at nominal sums to friendly agent-trustee-owners John Gordon, a wealthy English Catholic from Carolina, and Jesse Fish, for nine years a factor in St. Augustine of the Walton Exporting Company of New York. To Gordon the Spaniards sold the episcopal residence, situated at the southeast corner of today's King and St. George streets, which had been used on occasion by resident auxiliary bishops from Cuba; the Franciscan Convent of the Immaculate Conception; and, north of the presidio, the Mission Nombre de Dios with its hermitage of Nuestra Señora de la Leche y Buen Parto. To Fish the Spanish church officials conveyed the property and walls of the unfinished parish church, together with the Tolomato stone church building situated about five miles north of Nombre de Dios. According to plan, the agents would then sell the church properties to individuals of the English government at the highest possible prices. Puente completed these transactions two months prior to the eighteen-month deadline for such exchanges stipulated in the Treaty of Paris. Within a year, however, the churchmen, by that time in Cuba, heard the distressing news that Great Britain, taking a strict interpretation of the *patronato real*, the royal patronage relationship of church and state favored by Spain, had determined that the properties in question had been owned originally, not by the church, but by the Spanish Crown, and hence were public property already passed by escheat to British ownership in the treaty. To their dismay, the former St. Augustine church officials learned that the

1. This decline can be reviewed in Michael V. Gannon, *The Cross in the Sand: The Early Catholic Church in Florida* (Gainesville, Fla., 1965), chap. 5, "Decline and Ruin, 1675–1763," pp. 68–83; and in John Jay Tepaske, *The Governorship of Spanish Florida, 1700–1763* (Durham, N.C., 1964), chap. 7, "The Governor and the Church," pp. 160–91.

episcopal residence would be given over for use by the recusant Church of England, or Anglicans; that the Franciscan monastery would be made over into a military barracks; that the hermitage of La Leche would be converted into a hospital; and that the site of the new parish church building would be leveled to serve as an extension of the parade ground.[2] Later, in 1773, their former hospital-church of Nuestra Señora de la Soledad, situated south of the plaza, would be taken over for use as the Anglican parish church. The coquina structure was renamed St. Peter's and was embellished with a wooden spire, clock, and bells.[3]

Where were the former Spanish church officials? They were mostly in Cuba, some in New Spain, along with the former Spanish populations of *La Florida* and all the movable church possessions from St. Augustine, Apalache, and Pensacola. St. Augustine's sacred articles reached Havana in February 1764 via the schooner *Nuestra Señora de la Luz y Santa Bárbara*. On board were all of the town's altars, images, vestments, canopies, vessels, candlesticks, bells, and other sacred objects. Included, too, were fifteen folio volumes of parish registers (notations of baptisms, marriages, burials, etc.) that formed a continuous record of the pioneer Christian community from 1594 to the day of embarkation. The registers were placed in the archives of the Bishop of Santiago de Cuba, where they would remain for the next 143 years. Although freedom of worship had been promised them by the newly occupying English government, the Spanish populations of St. Augustine, Apalache, and Pensacola abandoned Florida almost completely. Their longtime antipathy toward England, together with offers from Charles III of new homes in Cuba and Mexico, would be incentive enough for the mass exodus. No doubt their mistrust of the English pledge to respect the free exercise of Roman Catholicism also played a part in their decision to withdraw. By March 1764, over three thousand people had debarked at Havana. The pastor of St. Augustine, Don Juan Joseph Solana, with his acting chief sacristan, was the last to leave San Agustin. The St. Augustine seculars resettled in Cuba and New Spain, most taking positions in and around Havana. The ten remaining Florida Franciscans, including the chaplains of San

2. Robert L. Gold, *Borderland Empires in Transition: The Triple-Nation Transfer of Florida* (Carbondale and Edwardsville, Ill., 1969), pp. 41–42, 138–39; Gannon, *Cross in the Sand*, pp. 84–86.

3. J. Leitch Wright, *Florida in the American Revolution* (Gainesville, Fla., 1975), p. 8.

Marcos de Apalache, also moved to Cuba in search of new assignments. The secular clergy from Pensacola apparently sailed to Vera Cruz, New Spain. It is interesting that a large number of Florida Indians also sought refuge with the exiting Spaniards.

In the decades immediately prior to the Spanish withdrawal Spain had had little success in pacifying, much less in Christianizing, the interior tribes. With British colonies to the north and French colonies to the west competing with her for Indian alliances, Spain had been left by 1763 with only the Apalache in some kind of control. To her surprise, when news of the change of flags became widely known, non-Christian Indians, many of them previously hostile to Spain, sought permission to accompany the departing Spaniards. Officials at St. Augustine and Pensacola, however, decided to take only those families that had been baptized or had committed themselves to conversion. Altogether eighty-nine Yamassee men, women, and children departed St. Augustine for Havana under those terms. On their arrival, a lack of provisions and yellow fever struck the Yamassees hard and only fifty-five remained alive in 1766. Five Indians seem to have accompanied the Spanish garrison that left Apalache for Havana, but forty families of Yamassee Apalachinos sailed in the vessels from San Miguel de Pensacola to Vera Cruz. In 1765, they were resettled in the nearby town on Tempoala (now Tempoal), which was renamed San Carlos, and there they appear to have experienced the same calamities as had the *inmigrantes* in Cuba.[4]

When England acquired the Florida peninsula from Spain, she also received at the same time eastern Louisiana from France, with its principal settlement of Mobile. English suzerainty extended, therefore, from the peninsula westward as far as the Mississippi. Dividing this vast territory at the Chattahoochee River, England created two new royal colonies: East Florida with a capital at St. Augustine and West Florida with a capital at Pensacola. The western colony would greatly expand its northern boundary to take advantage of the French-originated fur trade. England now had to staff its new domains with the necessary church officials. These of course would be licensed clergymen of the Church of England, and Parliament initially designated four in number for service in Florida: the Reverend Mr. John Forbes arrived in St. Augustine as

4. The best account of the Spanish evacuation is in Gold, *Empires in Transition,* pp. 132–37, 140, 153–61.

minister on May 5, 1764, and he would remain in East Florida throughout the British occupation. His may not have been the first Anglican services in East Florida, however. That honor probably belonged to the ship chaplain who held prayer book services on board one of John Hawkins' ships anchored inside the St. Johns River in the summer of 1565.[5]

The Reverend William Dawson was appointed to Pensacola, but he would withdraw from that position in 1766 in order to accept a more attractive ministry at St. John's Parish in Colleton, South Carolina. The Reverend Samuel Hart spent one year at Mobile before transferring to Charleston in 1765 to serve as assistant minister of St. Michael's Church. The Reverend Michael Smith Clerk, destined for ministerial labors in Mobile, settled instead in Jamaica where he was given church facilities by the bishop of London.[6] The direct auspices under which these men set out for America were those of the bishop of London and of the Incorporated Society for the Propagation of the Gospel in Foreign Parts. The latter body cooperated with the bishop in examining and recommending candidates for foreign service. It also assisted in financial support, as similar missionary societies act on behalf of certain Christian denominations at the present time. The travel expenses and salaries of the clergymen were paid from the public treasury, however, in much the same way as the patronato real provided for the Spanish clergy. The bishop of London had theoretical authority over sacred matters in the American colonies, but his powers were exercised at great distance, leading many colonists on the Atlantic seaboard to complain that the colonies should have a bishop or bishops of their own so that jurisdiction might be more knowledgeable and direct and to provide for the administration of confirmation and holy orders to those seeking those sacraments on this side of the Atlantic.

Many Anglicans, and, as might be expected, the great majority of colonial Congregationalists, Presbyterians, and other evangelicals opposed the establishment of an American Anglican episcopate because of its obvious connection with the aristocracy. One proponent of the plan wrote in 1765: "Alas! The [Anglican] Southern

5. See William Morrison Robinson, Jr., *The First Coming to America of the Book of Common Prayer, Florida, July 1565* (Austin, Texas, 1965).
6. Gold, *Empires in Transition*, pp. 143–44, 147; Wright, *American Revolution*, p. 8.

Clergy, as far as I can learn, are really averse to it. They are now their own pastors." And the commissary of South Carolina declared: "The Principles of most of the Colonists in America are independent in Matters of Religion, as well as republican in those of Government. . . . I can venture to affirm that it wou'd be as unsafe for an American Bishop (if such be appointed) to come hither, as it is at present for a Distributor of the Stamps."[7]

John Forbes certainly was his own man at St. Augustine, where he held title to sacramental and preaching offices at the parish church until his departure for England in 1782. Most of his time, however, he expended on non-religious activities. He became a member of the town council in 1765, and afterwards served, at one time or another, as justice of the vice-admiralty court, acting chief justice, and treasurer of the council. Forbes managed to gain ownership of six thousand acres of farmland, which he worked with some sixty slaves, and large property holdings in the town, which during the Revolutionary years he rented out to loyalist refugees and to enemy prisoners on parole. The effective care of souls at St. Augustine fell eventually into other hands, particularly those of the Reverend John Leadbeater, who conducted services for St. Augustine's growing military and civilian population in the 1770s, and the Reverend John Kennedy, who took Leadbeater's place when the latter left for England because of ill health. Kennedy gave the most effective ministerial service during the war years. Another was the Reverend James Seymour from Augusta, Georgia, who took refuge in St. Augustine when his parish church was seized by patriots. At St. Augustine he would be very much at home in a parish where everyone, minister and laity alike, prayed fervently throughout the war for George III and a Tory victory. Still another Anglican minister, the Reverend John Fraser, appeared in East Florida during these years and led services for the English overseers and their families at Andrew Turnbull's indigo plantation at New Smyrna from 1769 until 1772, the year he died. Leadbeater and Kennedy irregularly saw to the overseers' religious needs in the years thereafter, until the collapse of the plantation in 1777.[8]

In West Florida, the principal Anglican establishment was at Pen-

7. See Carl Bridenbaugh, *Mitre and Sceptre: Transatlantic Faith, Ideas, Personalities, and Politics* (New York, 1962), p. 249.
8. Wright, *American Revolution*, pp. 8–9, 38; Gold, *Empires in Transition*, p. 148.

82 / Eighteenth-Century Florida and the Revolution

sacola. George Johnstone, the first governor, proposed in 1765 that a public subscription be opened for a suitable new church in the town. From his contingency funds he made a beginning by contributing £150, which was £50 more than the annual salary of William Dawson, who was the minister at that time. It was hoped by Johnstone and his town council that pew rentals would be sufficient to cover building maintenance. Nothing came of the project, however, and for the entire British Period, despite repeated pleas from the clergy, neither Pensacola nor Mobile managed to erect a church for Anglican worship. Instead, the largest structure in each of the towns was employed to house both church and governmental activities. An insight into the inadequacy of these arrangements is provided in an official report to the Board of Trade in London, wherein unfavorable comparisons were made with church facilities then under construction in neighboring Spanish Louisiana: "To see the Fortifications, Churches, Hospitals, and Public Buildings, which are everywhere erecting in the Spanish Dominions, since the arrival of Don Antonio de Ulloa whilst nothing is undertaken on our part is extremely mortifying. . . . We have not even any place of Worship for asking the Blessing of Providence on our Endeavors."[9] Evidently the ministers were frequently in need of necessary communion plate and church furnishings, which a less than generous home government either failed to send or else sent as loans rather than as gifts.

When Samuel Hart departed Mobile for Charleston in 1765, and William Dawson abandoned the church at Pensacola in the year following, West Florida was left for a time without a resident licensed minister. Thomas Wilkinson, an unlicensed military chaplain, filled in for a short period at Mobile, and less regularly for the six hundred Anglican souls at Pensacola. Mobile received a new pastor in the person of the Reverend William Gordon, who arrived in 1763 and would stay until 1783. The Reverend Nathaniel Cotton took Dawson's place at Pensacola in 1768, but died three years later. Unfortunately, Pensacola did not enjoy a reputation for being a healthy environment for body, and perhaps not one for soul. When the Reverend George Chapman was appointed to succeed Cotton, he declined, saying that a man of his age and frailty would not have

9. Governor and Council of West Florida to the Board of Trade, 22 Nov. 1766; quoted ibid., p. 145.

"the smallest Chance of living six weeks at Pensacola."[10] Gordon, at Mobile, was not similarly daunted, and he applied for the position. The town council turned him down on grounds that he was a poor preacher. Still, Gordon did come over to conduct services at Pensacola from time to time in the nine years that intervened before the Spanish forces of Governor Bernardo de Gálvez began the capture of West Florida in 1780. It is remarkable that the bishop of London and the Gospel Propagation Society allowed the capital town of one of England's largest colonies to remain for so long a period without a resident pastor, and it suggests that what historian Carl Bridenbaugh said about Anglican negligences elsewhere in the colonies might be said here: "It was the hierarchy of the Church of England, managing an ecclesiastical empire without the knowledge of the most vital facts, for they displayed an ignorance of religious conditions and systems in the colonies, that made such blunders possible. . . . The Church of England must, therefore, share with the English political system, Parliament, and the Crown the responsibility for the loss of the colonies."[11]

If Florida Anglicanism was not particularly noted for its spiritual zeal or material accomplishments, it does deserve notice for its unfailing respect for the freedom of worship guarantees incorporated in the Treaty of Paris.[12] It is to the Church of England that Florida is indebted for the introduction of this most intimate of freedoms, and it is glory enough for any faith to have planted the principles of liberty in Florida soil, and to have nurtured the growth of those principles with such success that even the Spanish return in 1784 would not extinguish them altogether. To the aboriginal Indian tribes (whom the Church of England, like the Spanish settlers in their latter days, made no special attempt to evangelize), to the assorted white Presbyterians and Congregationalists, and to the few Jews, usually West Florida merchants, the Anglican communion extended the fullest rights of assembly for religious purposes. That freedom was extended in the most difficult direction as well, namely, to Roman Catholics. French residents of West Florida were almost all Catholics; the majority lived at Mobile where they had their own church building—the only one in West Florida—and Capuchin priests to celebrate mass in the years

10. Ibid., p. 147.
11. Bridenbaugh, *Mitre and Sceptre*, pp. 337–38.
12. See Gannon, *Cross in the Sand*, p. 84.

1763 to 1771 and again in 1777. The British authorities at Pensacola refused to accept fiscal responsibility for Catholic activities at Mobile, and there was certainly no legal cause for them to do so, but it is not recorded that they made any attempts to subvert or hinder the operation of Catholic institutions.

The most striking example of English respect for the freedom of religion came at New Smyrna in East Florida. There in 1768 1,255 male and female indentured servants, the great majority from Catholic Minorca, then under English rule, were put to work on Turnbull's infamous indigo plantation. English authorities permitted Dr. Turnbull to establish the Minorcans' pastor, Padre Pedro Camps, and an Augustinian assistant, Bartolome Casanovas, in full charge of the religious life of the Catholics and Greek Orthodox. Camps was able to communicate to church authorities in Havana through the agency of visiting Cuban fishermen, and his messages revealed that his people worshipped freely in a commodious brick church, dedicated under the name San Pedro, which contained a high altar, a centrally placed figure of Christ, and statues of Saints Peter and Anthony.

Although the plantation was ill fated from the start, and hundreds of laborers died over the next nine years from disease, malnutrition, and bad treatment, only Turnbull's local administration made attempts directly to hinder Father Camps' ministry. When in 1777 Governor Patrick Tonyn learned at St. Augustine of the injustices suffered by the Minorcans, he disbanded the colony and permitted the Catholic population with their pastor to take refuge in the capital, where many of the Minorcans' descendants still live today.[13] In sum, it can be said that, while the Spanish church suffered a variety of socioeconomic losses in the transfer of Florida to England, and certain of her communicants experienced deprivation and abuse at the hands of individual Englishmen, overall the Roman Catholic faith was allowed free exercise, even governmental protection, and no special burdens were placed on its ecclesiastical institutions other than the requirements made of all faiths, to declare their property, revenues, claims, and personnel.

In the course of the American Revolution, Spain threw in her lot with the patriots and launched attacks against West Florida out of New Orleans, capturing Mobile in 1780, and Pensacola a year later.

13. The best account of the Minorcan experience is Jane Quinn, *Minorcans in Florida: Their History and Heritage* (St. Augustine, Fla., 1975).

Religion in the British and Second Spanish Periods / 85

Soon it had control of the entire colony, and in the peace treaty signed in 1783 that ended the war between England and the nascent United States, East Florida, too, was ceded back to its original possessors. The exchange was as difficult for the English Floridians as it had been for the Spaniards twenty years before. Most of the 16,000 dispossessed loyalists left for new homes in the British West Indies, Nova Scotia, the Bahamas, or elsewhere. The exodus was as painful for the ministers as it was for the rest, and some, such as John Forbes and James Seymour, died soon after.[14] By terms of the new treaty British subjects who wished to remain in the Floridas were advised that they must become Roman Catholics. Various associations of loyalists negotiated with the Spanish ambassador in London in order to obtain articles of religious toleration, but in vain: Spain was determined to have the same religious unity in her colonies as she possessed at home.[15] As will be seen, that determination was never realized in fact. And despite the recalcitrant Spanish position in the matter, large numbers of Englishmen elected to remain in the Floridas and see what happened. A goodly number lived in and around St. Augustine, and others settled the farmsteads along the St. Johns and St. Marys rivers.

When Governor Vizente Manuel de Zéspedes arrived at St. Augustine on July 12, 1784, with 500 troops and a community of civilians from Havana, he may have expected to impose religious uniformity on the province given him. And this may have been the expectation, too, of the long-suffering Minorcans, whose ailing pastor, Pedro Camps, solemnized the Spanish repossession with a mass. But such was not to be. The population was too disparate. There were too many Englishmen, Scots, Swiss, and American frontiersmen from the new states to permit homogenization of any sort, at any level. And there was too heady a sense of independence in the air, including the spirit of religious toleration, which would not be denied. Recognizing this, the governors of the two Spanish Floridas had to seek new solutions for the religious problems confronting them, and the bishops had to look beyond Spain itself for priests who could serve in the new circumstances.

Already before the retrocession, in 1778, thanks to initiatives taken by Father Camps while still at New Smyrna and communicating with church officials at Havana through Cuban fishing fleets,

14. Wright, *American Revolution*, p. 132.
15. Ibid., pp. 123–24.

the Spanish Crown had appointed two young Irish priests for service in the English province: Fathers Thomas Hassett and Michael O'Reilly, natives of Longford, Ireland, who had just completed studies at the Irish College at Salamanca. The Revolution had prevented the two clerics from reaching their destination until shortly after cession of Florida back to Spain. Now, as Spain envisioned it, their work would be to concentrate on bringing English and American frontiersmen into the True Faith. But the state of Catholicity in St. Augustine itself so shocked Hassett that he knew his mission to the English-speaking settlers would have to await improvements in the capital's own religious life. A chapel fitted out by Father Camps on the ground floor of a residence near the city gate had served the Minorcans since 1777 and was still the sole place of Catholic worship when Hassett arrived. The Irishman thought it "wretched" and "lacking in all things appropriate for the celebration of the divine liturgy."[16] The former hospital-church of La Soledad, lately called St. Peters, had been gutted by the departing English and was, in the words of one royal engineer, a "useless pile of masonry."[17] The Franciscan monastery was no longer good for anything but barracks, but then, the Franciscans having been denied reentrance into Florida, it might as well serve the purpose to which the English had converted it. The Episcopal residence had been improved under British rule, and Hassett decided therefore to open his parish church in the upper story of that fifty-by-ninety-foot masonry building. As for altar furnishings, Hassett reported to his superiors, "The things found here in the hands of the priest of the Minorcans [Pedro Camps] are so few and in such poor condition that they are practically useless, almost as bad as having nothing."[18] By the time St. Augustine had a decent church building in which its residents—Spaniards, Minorcans, English-speaking converts, and others—could worship, Hassett would be far away in a new assignment. It would be his companion, Father Michael O'Reilly, who in the years 1792–97 would supervise the construction and dedication of the parish church whose facade and lateral walls still stand today fronting the old plaza. When completed it would be the most splendid church in the Floridas, as it also would be, it must be said, the only truly notable accomplishment of the Roman Catholic

16. See Gannon, *Cross in the Sand*, p. 92.
17. Ibid.
18. Ibid.

church in East Florida during the Second Spanish Period. The only other claimant for that honor could be a Hassett-sponsored school for Minorcan children, apparently the first free school in what is now the United States, which remained open for thirty-five years following its foundation in 1787.

In West Florida the restoration of Roman Catholic authority quickly followed the Spanish occupation forces. Father Salvador de la Esperanza, a religious order priest, took over the church at Mobile in March, 1780, and shortly afterwards the military commander of the town renamed the parish *La Purissimo Concepcion* (Immaculate Conception) by which name the pioneer parish, now a cathedral, is still known today. Esperanza was replaced by Dominican Father Francisco Notario in 1782. Mobile under Spanish rule was again the only town in West Florida to possess a church building, although, in 1784, it was reported to be in a state of disrepair.[19] Capuchin Father Pedro Valez was the first priest to assume parochial responsibilities in Pensacola following the surrender of the capital. For many years he and his successors would have to conduct services in an *almacén*, or warehouse.

The size of these and other West Florida communities is given in a 1785 report: Pensacola had 300 inhabitants; Mobile, 746; Baton Rouge, 270; and Natchez, 1,550. Three years later, Mobile had doubled its population, Baton Rouge had tripled, and Natchez had increased to 2,679. By the latter date there was also in existence a settlement at Tensaw River, forty-five miles outside Mobile, and another, Manchac, at the mouth of the Iberville, which between them numbered 800 or 900 people.[20] Obviously, these increases were due to the influx of Anglo-Americans. This high concentration of Protestants and other non-Catholics also presented church authorities with a new problem, unlike any that had been met before in Spain's American domains. During the first Florida occupation the Spanish church had had the twin responsibilities of providing religious services for Spanish military and civilian populations, and of sending missionaries into the interior to evangelize the aborigines. Now Spain faced a different set of tasks: to reduce Spanish, French, and Irish priests, secular and regular, to some kind

19. See Lyman P. Powell, *Historic Towns of the Southern States* (Boston, Mass., 1900), pp. 348–50.
20. These figures from 1785 and 1788 are cited in Charles Gayarre, *History of Louisiana* (New York, 1903), p. 170.

of ecclesiastical unity under the patronato real, and to appease or convert the Anglo-American settlers who were becoming so numerous it was not reasonable to expect that Spain could keep them out of her unguarded territories on grounds that they did not pay allegiance to the correct mitred hierarchy.

That hierarchy in the beginning of the Second Spanish Period was centered still at Havana, where the two Floridas were comprised under the jurisdiction of Bishop Santiago José de Echevarría y Elquezúa. It was not expected that Bishop Echevarría would have direct, or even accurate, knowledge of the souls under his care, since his domains included not only Cuba and the Floridas, but the whole of Louisiana territory north as far as the Illinois country. He therefore delegated much of his authority to priests who were already in the areas. Capuchin Father Cyril de Barcelona was designated *vicar forane* for all the parishes in Louisiana and West Florida. In 1784, he was elevated to auxiliary bishop with residence in New Orleans. In East Florida Echevarría named Father Hassett as vicar, with responsibility for the entire population, which Governor Zéspedes described in 1787 as follows: "900 white persons of all ages and both sexes and 490 slaves. Of the white people, thirty-one are natives of Spain, twenty-five of the Canary Islands, sixty-two Floridians, 448 Minorcans, Italians and Greeks; and 339 Britons who have been taken under the King's protection."[21]

In 1787, the Holy See at Rome divided Echevarría's diocese to form the new Diocese of San Cristobal, with its see at Havana, to which a Cuban priest, José de Trespalacios y Verdeja, was appointed as first bishop. Louisiana and the Floridas now fell under the jurisdiction of San Cristobal. Later, in 1795, the vicar general of Havana, Luis Ignacio Peñalver y Cardenas, was consecrated bishop of a newly erected Diocese of Louisiana, with a see at New Orleans, into which both East and West Florida were placed.[22] This diocese was beset by almost continuous internal conflict and turmoil, most of it generated by petty arguments over jurisdiction.[23]

21. Vizente Manuel de Zéspedes to José Gálvez, 12 May 1787, Papeles procedentes de la Isla de Cuba (North Carolina Historical Commission), cited in Thomas J. Burns, "The Catholic Church in West Florida, 1783–1850" (Master's thesis, Florida State University, 1962), p. 23.
22. For these changes in ecclesiastical jurisdiction see Gannon, *Cross in the Sand*, pp. 96, 110.
23. The best account of this strife is given in Burns, "Church in West Florida," chap. 3, "Intra-Ecclesiastical Controversies," pp. 43–79.

Religion in the British and Second Spanish Periods / 89

It is remarkable, given the uncertain sound that emanated from the church's trumpet at New Orleans, that any church work at all was done in the Floridas. But somehow, as in the earlier Anglican experience, the local ministries survived despite poor leadership and the Gospel continued to be preached. That part of the Floridas which today forms the American state would not receive its own resident Roman Catholic bishop until 1858. Before that date it would be the stepchild of New Orleans, and later of Mobile and of Charleston.

What did this relatively remote church authority decide to do about the problem posed by the influx of Anglo-Americans? About the only thing it could do, in cooperation with the Crown and the two governors, was to encourage Irish clergy to undertake special missionary work among the English-speaking frontiersmen. There was no real expectation that either church or state could enforce credal uniformity. In 1789, Governor-General Esteban Miró of West Florida observed: "The king has sent his royal order that settlers from Kentucky and other settlements 'whose rivers empty into the Ohio' may come and establish themselves, provided that non-Catholics have their religious rites in private."[24] The king had added his wish that schools be set up for the settlers' children so that they might be instructed in the True Faith at an early age, but at the same time he cautioned that there be no requirement that the children be baptized.

In the same year Miró published a decree that formally introduced a measure of religious liberty into West Florida.[25] To Colonel James Robertson, founder of Nashville, he wrote: "I can assure you that you will find here your welfare, without being either molested on religious matters, or paying any duty."[26] Without question this limited policy of religious toleration was an expedient expressly designed to attract an immigrant population into Spain's frontier districts. The ultimate aim was that Irish missionaries, exercising "sweet persuasion, proper and exemplary conduct, complete avoidance of discord and partisanship," would lead the Anglo-American

24. Miró to Josef Valliere (commander at Natchez), 28 Feb. 1789, Papeles procedentes de Cuba, ibid., p. 41.
25. See Jack D. L. Holmes, "Spanish Religious Policy in West Florida: Enlightened or Expedient?" *Journal of Church and State*, vol. 15, no. 2 (1973): 262.
26. Miró to Robertson, New Orleans, 20 Apr. 1789; quoted ibid., p. 263.

youth into the Roman Catholic faith.[27] Indeed, royal decrees of May 14, 1790, and November 30, 1792, stressed the fact that the grant of free worship was temporary only.[28] In the end the policy failed of its purposes, as not only did few settlers opt for the Catholic faith, but some Catholic Spaniards, attracted by the relaxed standards of credal affiliation, separated themselves from the full practice of that faith.[29] Still it was an enlightened policy for Spain to adopt, and one is impressed by nineteenth-century historian John F. H. Clairborne's conclusion that "There was, in fact, more religious freedom and toleration for Protestants in the Natchez district than Catholics, and dissenters from the ruling denomination, enjoyed in either Old or New England."[30]

Miró and his counterpart in East Florida, Zéspedes, were asked to submit reports on the numbers of Anglo-Americans in their districts and to propose specific plans for the erection of special missionary parishes among them. To that end both governors went on tour to see for themselves. Miró was particularly impressed by the growth he discovered in the Natchez area, which was situated at the confluence of three creeks, Catherine's, Second, and Cole's. Using the creeks as boundaries, he proposed a parish and church building at Catherine's Creek, with a mission eighteen miles away on Cole's. The Tensaw River settlement also suggested itself as a likely parish site: there were fifty-nine American families living there, a total of 366 people.

Miró's next step on returning to his capital was to secure English-speaking Irish clergy. After lengthy negotiations he succeeded in recruiting four from Spain, where, like Hassett and O'Reilly in East Florida, they had studied theology in the Colegio de Irlandeses at Salamanca. Their names were Gregory White, Constantine McKenna, Michael Lamport, and William Savage, and later records from the 1790s indicate not only that they served in the posts assigned them but that they achieved considerable good for their religion. Six more Irishmen were sent to Louisiana in 1792, including the Capuchin Francis Lennan, who would have a very active

27. Miró Conde de Gálvez (Bernardo de Gálvez), New Orleans, 5 Sept. 1785, quoted ibid., p. 262.
28. See ibid., pp. 264–65.
29. See Arthur P. Whitaker, *The Mississippi Question, 1795–1803: A Study in Trade, Politics and Diplomacy* (New York, 1934), p. 182.
30. John F. H. Clairborne, *Mississippi as a Province, Territory and State* (Jackson, Miss., 1880), pp. 136–37.

career in West Florida until 1813.[31] Perhaps more tolerant of denominational differences and of the principles of civil liberty than would be clergy of Iberian extraction, the Irishmen in the West Florida wilderness accommodated themselves to the spirit of the place and times.

But Bishop Peñalver, of more conservative mind, was clearly distressed by the scene that he surveyed in 1799: "Emigration from the western part of America and toleration of the sects have attracted to this colony a gang of adventurers who acknowledge no God and have no religion. . . . They have made the morals of our people much worse by their conduct. . . . The people in the parishes who formerly displayed an attachment to religion are losing their faith and their customs; compliance with the Easter precepts decreases and people turn a deaf ear to the admonitions of the clergy."[32] The situation would not change in Peñalver's favor. When one reflects on the political and social background of West Florida at that time, the problems faced by civil government in law, population planning, finance, trade and commerce, the encouragement by the United States of frontier intrigue, and the near uncontrollable movements of land-hungry American backwoodsmen, it would have been folly to expect that Spain, weakened in both military and ecclesiastical influence, would have been able, even through the instrumentality of Irish clergy, to turn the clock back to simpler times. In Pensacola itself one could read the signs. The state of religion was in ruinous condition, as was the town itself. Many parishioners had not confessed their sins for as long as five years; in 1790, only seven Catholics received Holy Communion during the Easter season, which was one of the grave precepts of the church. As the parish moved into the nineteenth century, its few remaining worshippers attended mass in the same old leaky almacén, or warehouse. The age of Roman Catholic dominance in West Florida was slowly and painfully ebbing away.

In East Florida similar efforts were made to reach the Anglo-Americans. Father Hassett went north in 1790 to do what missionary work he could among the families settled on the St. Johns, St.

31. See Jack D. L. Holmes, "Father Francis Lennan and His Activities in Spanish Louisiana and West Florida," *Louisiana Studies*, vol. 5, no. 4, pp. 255-68.
32. Dispatch of 30 July 1799, translated in James Alexander Robertson, ed., *Louisiana under the Rule of Spain, France and the United States, 1785-1807*, 2 vols. (Cleveland, Ohio, 1911), 1:355.

Marys and Nassau rivers. Traveling a distance of six hundred miles over a period of five weeks, the St. Augustine pastor found many men and women who had never seen a priest before, nor even a Protestant minister, in their entire lives. From family to family of these newcomers from Georgia and the Carolinas Hassett trudged, instructing children and adults in the fundamentals of Christian doctrine. To all the families he gave Roman Catholic catechisms in the English language that had been printed in New York at the Spanish king's expense. He also personally gave instructions that were received so eagerly in some places that Hassett was able to baptize seventy-eight children and fifty-one black slaves before ending his journey.[33] The experience led him to press for the assignment to East Florida of more Irish clergy, and in December 1791, three such missionaries arrived at St. Augustine. None of them would ever reach their intended posts among the northern settlers, however, as sickness forced the withdrawal of all three.

The erection of frontier parishes never got beyond the planning stage, and to the great regret of Hassett, O'Reilly, and their successors at St. Augustine during the remainder of the Second Spanish Period, thousands of frontiersmen continued to live out their days without baptism and the consolations of religion. Again the cumbersome operation of the patronato real, the routine, if not stagnant, political administration, and the impoverished state of the province as a whole resulted in lost opportunity. The formation of an active English Catholic colony in Florida to rival those in Maryland and New York, which seemed possible to Hassett in 1790, never materialized. And Catholic life continued to contract around the tired town of St. Augustine. In East Florida, as in West, other churches and other people were waiting in the wings.

33. See Gannon, *Cross in the Sand*, p. 101.

Commentary

KENNETH COLEMAN

BOTH British Florida and Georgia had small populations and had to begin their economies after their creation as colonies. Georgia at the end of twenty years had roughly five thousand people, while the Floridas had perhaps eight thousand by 1775 before the influx of loyalists from other southern colonies swelled this figure. There were two major differences between Georgia and the Floridas: the former had no hostile enemy like Spain just beyond its borders and no unnatural influx of loyalists from the other southern colonies after 1775. Georgia's earliest population came directly from Europe, from England, Scotland, and two German areas, while most of the population of the British Floridas came from other American colonies. The Florida area was better known in 1763, especially the territory in and around St. Augustine, than was the Georgia area in 1733. Florida had a much more rapid growth in the two decades under the British than it had experienced in the two centuries under the Spanish. There was little agricultural development during the First Spanish Period, especially after the decline of the missions.

To look at religion in eighteenth-century Florida as Professor Michael Gannon has, one must realize that almost all of the Spanish population had left Florida in 1763 and 1764, and new beginnings were necessary. The original decision to fund four clergymen at £100 out of the parliamentary grant for the Floridas was more liberal than Georgia's original treatment had been. Of course, Georgia was not founded as a royal colony and only received a parliamentary subsidy when she became royal in 1754. The cooperation of the Society for the Propagation of the Gospel in Foreign Parts and the bishop of London in securing Anglican clergymen for the Floridas was no less than it had been for other colonies in this period, including Georgia. The youth of colonial clergymen and their poor pay frequently resulted in short stays and transfers to better positions. Professor Gannon notes that this was the case for Dawson, Hart, and Clerk in their moves from Florida to South Carolina and to Jamaica. The strange thing about Anglican clergymen in the Floridas is the indication that their entire salary was paid by Parliament. In Georgia in the royal period, after 1754, pay came from the parliamentary grant and even from the parish in one instance. Perhaps some of these same sources were used by Florida clergymen. Besides there were glebes granted to clergymen in Georgia. There is some evidence that they were also granted in Florida, although Professor Gannon does not mention this in his paper.

There is similarity in the activities of the Reverend John Forbes in St. Augustine and the Reverend Bartholomew Zouberbuhler in Georgia. Both were important citizens, held secular offices, and were also substantial planters. Each could have justified his planting upon the need for additional income, and they probably received better attention as clerics as a result of these secular activities. With Zouberbuhler this did not mean that he neglected his clerical duties as was true of the Reverend Forbes. Zouberbuhler's plantations provided income with which he paid a catechist to instruct Negro slaves in Christianity. This was the major missionary work for slaves that was carried on in colonial Georgia.

The Reverend James Seymour evidently went from Augusta, Georgia, to St. Augustine in late 1780 or 1781. By his own statement, he remained in Augusta throughout the period of Whig control of Georgia (1776-78) and on into 1780. Even when Augusta was under Whig control he was left alone, although he did stop holding public services because of Whig objections to "Tory" religion. Such treatment by the local Whigs makes it clear that Mr. Seymour was respected by many in Augusta despite his lack of sympathy for the American cause. More such clergymen in frontier colonies would have given the Anglican church a better reputation than it enjoyed in America by 1775.

It was not particularly remarkable that for much of the time that it served as the capital of West Florida, Pensacola had no Anglican

Commentary / 95

clergyman or church. It seems fairly typical that no clergyman wanted to go to this small and new colony or to its "God-forsaken" capital. Savannah's first church was not begun until 1744 and not completed until 1750, seventeen years after the colony was founded. Savannah frequently had no Anglican clergyman in its first twenty years. Augusta was in worse condition for the entire colonial period, even after the parishioners built a church at their own expense in 1749. There were only two really operational Anglican parishes, Savannah and Augusta, in Georgia at the end of the colonial period when the population of the colony was fifty thousand. The Floridas' situation was like that of Georgia.

Toleration by British and Anglicans of dissenters, Roman Catholics, and Jews was normal in the colonies by the 1760s; hence such toleration in Florida was not unusual. There is the question of whether the Anglican church in either East or West Florida was established as an official church. Professor Gannon has not provided an answer to this query, nor has he given any indication that there were dissenting clergymen present in either of the British Floridas. There were probably many dissenters who came from the other southern colonies. There is a record in August 1765 of a £75 payment to French Protestants at Mobile in Clinton N. Howard's *The British Development of West Florida* (Berkeley and Los Angeles, 1947). One might wonder if there were not British dissenters in East or West Florida during this period also. Perhaps it was either the abnormality of the war years or the lack of adequate records which makes it impossible to answer this question. One might also wonder after listening to Professor Gannon's paper why the Spanish Crown appointed Irish priests such as Fathers Thomas Hassett and Michael O'Reilly, rather than Spanish prelates, to officiate in the British Floridas.

The fact that Hassett was confined mainly to the St. Augustine area and was unable to minister to Americans and Englishmen in the area north of East Florida was not unusual considering the transportation difficulties and the lack of available clergymen in Florida. When John Wesley came to Georgia his plan was to do missionary work among the Indians, but, because there was no Anglican priest in Savannah during this period in Georgia, he was unable to. This was also the case with Zouberbuhler, who was prevented from officiating in Georgia parishes which had no Anglican clergymen by prior obligations. One man could do only so much,

96 / Eighteenth-Century Florida and the Revolution

and he had to take care of the needs of his own parish first. Most colonies were not so fortunate as was South Carolina where the Reverend Charles Woodmason was able to officiate in the upcountry.

The deteriorating conditions of the Roman Catholic church in Florida after the Spanish returned in 1783 was to be expected. The Spanish missions had disappeared many decades earlier. The clergy, church, and government which operated in the eighteenth century had little of the missionary zeal that had existed earlier. Much of Florida's settled area was more like the Georgia–South Carolina frontier than anything that had existed in Florida before.

The little work that Father Hassett did in the St. Johns–St. Marys river area illustrates the desire for religion—any type of religion—among many American frontiersmen. For people with no Roman Catholic background to receive Father Hassett's instructions gladly showed their desire for religious instruction. This is indicative of the interdenominational character of much of the religious life on the American frontier. Father Hassett may have been trying to convert the people to Catholicism, but perhaps he realized that he could accomplish little in this regard and was instead trying to do whatever he could for the totally unchurched. Again this was similar to what other clergymen did on the British colonial and United States frontiers.

Since the Anglo-Americans in the Floridas were like the dissenters in the English colonies, any religious uniformity or establishment similar to that in the home country was impossible. This was true even in Spanish territory, regardless of the attitude and hopes of the European authorities or those in older American areas like Cuba. Clearly Father Hassett realized this, and other religious and secular officials did also.

For both the British and Second Spanish periods there is the question of why the church was able to accomplish so little in Florida. Certainly this small accomplishment was influenced by the eighteenth-century attitude which expected an officially established church to operate with support from the government, and usually there was little or no congregational financial aid. It was simply not considered the business of the people in the colony to support the church financially. Parish loyalties of the few clergymen present were a part of this establishment and an indication of the localism so often felt in rural America. The difficulties of travel in frontier areas have already been noted. Certainly the hard condition of life in new colonies made many people give first priority to making a living for the here and now rather than preparing for the hereafter. The unsettled life-style of the Floridians in both periods also had its effect. Churches generally do better in established societies than in frontier areas. This is clear enough from the entire religious history of the British colonies in America.

There has been no family study for Georgia as Professor Corbett has done for the St. Augustine area of East Florida during the Second Spanish Period. Hence, I am unable to draw parallels with Georgia as I did in the case of Professor Gannon's subject. The census, which was the main source of Corbett's paper, did not include the St. Johns–St. Marys river area of East Florida, where comparison with Georgia would be most obvious and fruitful. This is unfortunate, but historians are bound by their sources. But some comparisons can be made as to the nationalities and the types of population in the St. Augustine area and in Georgia during the colonial period. Four major groups of white settlers have been delineated in East Florida, and there were four main national groups in early Georgia. They were the English, Scots, Germans, and Americans from other colonies. The latter were mainly Scotch-Irish and English in their backgrounds. A few colonists came to Georgia from the British West Indies, but most Americans had come from the Carolinas and from Virginia. Some New Englanders came south immediately after the American Revolution. In Georgia by 1790 most settlers had been in America for such a long time that the national groups were not very distinct, a condition which did not exist for Florida in the same period.

The greatest difference between Georgia and Florida residential patterns was in the proportion of the settlers who lived in the St. Augustine area and the importance of that city to the colony. As late as 1790 the Savannah area was not nearly so important to Georgia. True, the wealthiest rice planters in Georgia had homes there, and most of the slaves were located on the coastal rice plantations. But by 1790, the great majority of Georgia's population were small-scale farmers who lived in the up-country. This made Augusta a town of increasing importance. These settlers were more like those in the St. Johns–St. Marys river area, and they had their counterparts in West Florida, especially along the Mississippi River. Many such people in the Floridas were Tories, who were more oriented towards the United States than towards Spain and who returned to the United States, or at least became more tolerant of it, as the hatreds of the war years abated. This attitude is obvious as late as the War of 1812 when settlers wished Florida to become a part of the United States.

A definite conclusion that can be derived from studying a segment of society in frontier areas is that the environment and the makeup of the settlers often had more to do with events than did the goals projected by home governments or the activities of resident officials who had been dispatched to the colony to carry out these plans. As James Habersham wrote in 1772 after some thirty years in Georgia: "It is easy for People in England to speculate and refine, but here [in Savannah] we must act as *Necessity requires*, which is an infallible Rule." Frontier historian Frederick Jackson Turner would hardly have been surprised at this statement or at this conclusion, nor should contemporary scholars and researchers.

Changing Traditions in
St. Augustine Architecture

ALBERT MANUCY

SPANISH building practice is the basic tradition of historic architecture in St. Augustine, but other factors—environmental, economic, political, and cultural—have greatly changed the face of the community during the four centuries of its existence. In this essay, we shall examine one important era of change: the impact of English building practice and neoclassicism upon St. Augustine construction during the chaotic last quarter of the 1700s. First, however, let me provide some background for the two major traditions, Spanish and English, which have met at St. Augustine and blended into a distinctive, vernacular style.

SPANISH TRADITION

According to laws enacted in 1563 and 1573, the formula for allocating real estate to settlers in the Americas was based upon the amount of land needed to sustain a foot soldier—that is, a peasant, or *peón*. The term for this quantity of land and its produce was *peonía*. After living on the land five years, the grantee gained free simple title. A gentleman—a *caballero*—having a horse and larger responsibilities, naturally required more support. His allotment, called a *caballería*, was about five times the size of a peonía.

The law specified that each new colony must comprise at least thirty settlers with the requisite livestock and a priest, all to be set within a municipal district not smaller than 144 square miles (see Fig. 1). In theory, at least, the municipality was autonomous and democratic: members of the town council, which was empowered

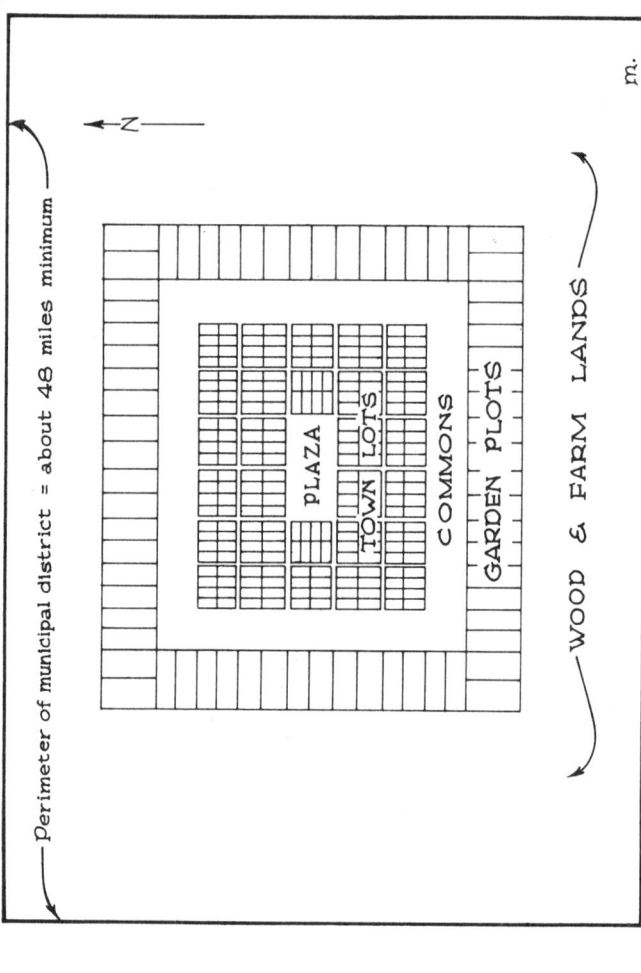

Fig. 1. This schematic plan for new colonies in Spanish America is based upon ordinances promulgated in 1563 by the Spanish Crown. See *Colección de documentos*, 8:512–31.

to grant lands, were chosen by the landholders themselves. Within each district was a village or town with a plaza, a church, public buildings, and individual town lots. Outside the town was the commons, or community pasture. Here each landholder was entitled to grazing space for his livestock. Next came the individual farm grants, each with at least three acres reserved for a garden plot. After all grants were made, one-fourth of the remaining land went to the conquistador of the region. The rest was set aside for future settlers.

Laying out a new town began with the plaza. Its size was proportionate to the number of settlers, but was not smaller than 200 by 300 feet. The street grid started at the plaza. Ideally there were ten streets coming into the plaza, two at each corner plus one more on each long side. Next came sites around the plaza for government buildings, the public market, and tradesmen's shops. The church either fronted on the plaza or was in a conspicuous location nearby. Other surrounding land was laid out in 50- by 100-foot units; the citizenry drew lots for these, beginning with the land closest to the plaza.[1]

Transposition of the traditional plaza to Spain's American colonies helps to account for the persistent "Spanishness" of many cities today. The plaza with street grid, however, was not a Spanish invention. It was in standard plans for Rome's colonies in the days of the empire and was revived during the twelfth century in Europe. This kind of planning, arbitrarily setting aside wide expanses of public space, was possible only in states with centralized political authority. Such was sixteenth-century Spain, an absolute monarchy bent upon instant development of New World resources, and whether the new community bloomed or withered, presumably the success potential was built into its plan.[2]

The extent to which Spain's ordinances of 1563 and 1573 actually affected the layout of St. Augustine has not, at this writing, been conclusively shown, but the fact remains that there is a central plaza with a grid of streets (see Fig. 2). The somewhat irregular placement of the streets as well as the inconsistencies in the dimensions of lots and blocks are traceable to such factors as the topog-

1. *Colección de documentos inéditos relativos al descubrimiento, conquista y organización de las antiguas posesiones españoles de América y Oceania* . . . (Madrid, 1864–84), 8:512–31.
2. Howard Saalman, *Medieval Cities* (New York, 1968), pp. 29–30, 114.

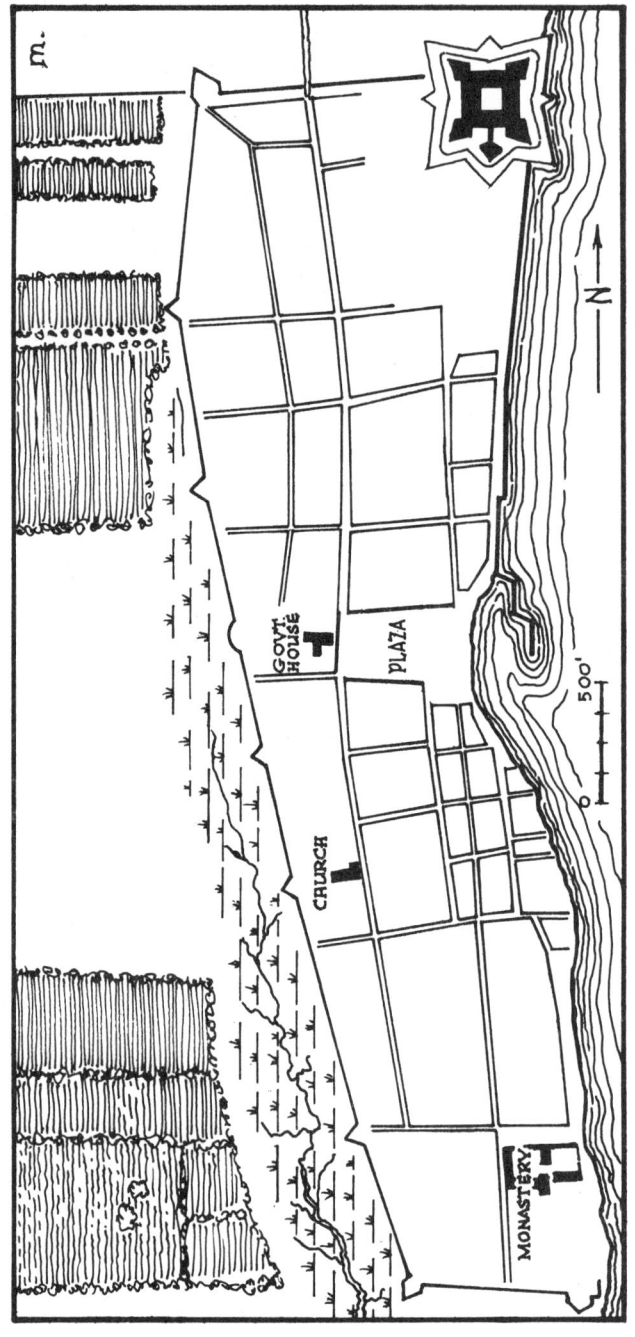

Fig. 2. The sketch, a plan of St. Augustine about 1764, is a simplification of Thomas Jefferys, *St. Augustine the Capital of East Florida* (London, 1769), library of the St. Augustine Historical Society.

Changing Traditions in St. Augustine Architecture / 103

raphy of the peninsular site, drastic turnovers in population with wholesale property transfers and abandonments, loss of records, collapse of fences and blurring of lot lines, not to mention the inevitable encroachments upon public land.

Despite two hundred years of Spanish occupation it is difficult to characterize St. Augustine architecture as "Spanish," any more than you can point to one of the regional styles in Spain and call it typical of all Spain. In appearance, the Asturian farmhouse differs from the great house-barn of Cataluña or the Andalucian hacienda to the same degree that a thatched cottage of Devonshire is unlike a rough stone dwelling on the Cornish coast. Yet the basic functions for all are the same. Each has evolved as the shelter and work base best suited to man's need in a special environment.

The same was true at St. Augustine. Environmental influences—hot sun tempered by ocean breezes and plentiful rainfall; the flat, sandy site bordered by estuarine marshes; an abundance of building materials such as timber, shell (for lime), shellstone and thatch (but no significant deposits of clay or iron)—were no less important in the evolution of a St. Augustine architecture than were imported building traditions and a struggling economy.

From the earliest palm-thatch hovels to shellstone-and-shingle, St. Augustine structures were indigenous and Spanish artisans were obliged to adapt traditional practice to available materials, with attendant structural changes. Graphic sources of the sixteenth century represent St. Augustine housing as timberframe with vertical board walling and thatch roof. There followed a progression to monolithic walls of the concrete called "tabby," which is a mix of lime and sand with shell aggregate, tamped into board forms. In some instances these walls contained a core of vertical poles or even the timberframe commonly used as reinforcement in Spain. Stone construction was almost unknown in St. Augustine before 1672. Native shellstone (*coquina*) had been reported as existing in 1580 and had been used experimentally, but, until the beginning of the Castillo (1672), stone walling was deemed too heavy for the light sandy soil with its high water table. When the English burned the town in 1702, aid from the king's treasury along with stone from his quarries (opened for building the Castillo in 1671) combined to usher in an era of stone housing. Walling was generally coursed, squared rubble, with lime-plastered surfaces. Both boarded timberframe and tabby continued, sometimes in combination with each other or with stone. Thatch roofs persisted; the vast majority of local buildings were thatched with straw or palm even as late as 1759. A few houses (twenty-six) were roofed with shingles or boards and fewer yet (twenty-three) had flat masonry roofs.³

Another important result of local influence, though less obvious than structural materials, was a floor plan well suited to the north Florida climate (see Fig. 3). Data on this plan are available from a 1788 map, from archeological studies, and from a few extant houses. That it was a characteristic feature of Spanish St. Augustine is also attested to by three separate observers in the early 1760s.⁴ The comments of this trio are important, inasmuch as each of them, as an alien to Spanish culture, found many things worthy of mention which Spanish writers ignored as commonplace. But because their fairly lengthy observations are readily available elsewhere, here I do no more than cite and discuss a few excerpts: John Bartram wrote "On the back side of the house or yard, where the chief entrance is (for few but the grand houses, except taverns, had street doors . . .) there is generally a terraced walk, with seats of the same 18 inches high next to the house wall, to sit down upon when weary of walking. The walks about 9 foot wide, with a staircase at one end of the chambers. . . ."⁵ William Stork noted that "before the entry of most of the houses runs a portico of stone arches,"⁶ and William De Brahm added that "entrances are shaded by Piazzas supported by Tuskan Pillars or Pillasters against the South Sun."⁷

    3. Boazio's original sketch depicting Drake's raid on St. Augustine (1586) is the earliest known representation of the local architecture. As an accurate record of the construction, its value is questionable due to the small scale of the drawing and other considerations. Two Spanish maps of slightly later date unmistakably picture board-and-thatch housing. They are reproduced in Verne E. Chatelain, *The Defenses of Spanish Florida, 1565–1763* (Washington, D.C., 1941): Map 3, Plano del fuerte biejo que está en San Agustín . . . and Map 4, Mapa del pueblo, fuerte y caño de San Agustín. . . . Thomas Cates' narrative of the 1586 raid states that the houses were wooden; see Albert Manucy, ed., *The History of Castillo de San Marcos and Fort Matanzas from Contemporary Narratives and Letters* (Washington, 1943), p. 7. See also idem, *The Houses of St. Augustine* (St. Augustine, 1962), pp. 15–33, 62–73, 99–112.

    4. A detailed discussion of house plans at St. Augustine is in Manucy, *Houses of St. Augustine*, pp. 48–61.

    5. John Bartram, *Diary of a Journey through the Carolinas, Georgia and Florida* . . . (Philadelphia, 1942), p. 52.

    6. William Stork, *A Description of East-Florida* . . . (London, 1765), p. 12.

    7. William G. De Brahm, "History of the Three Provinces, South Carolina, Georgia and East-Florida" (Harvard College Library MSS., 1771), p. 298.

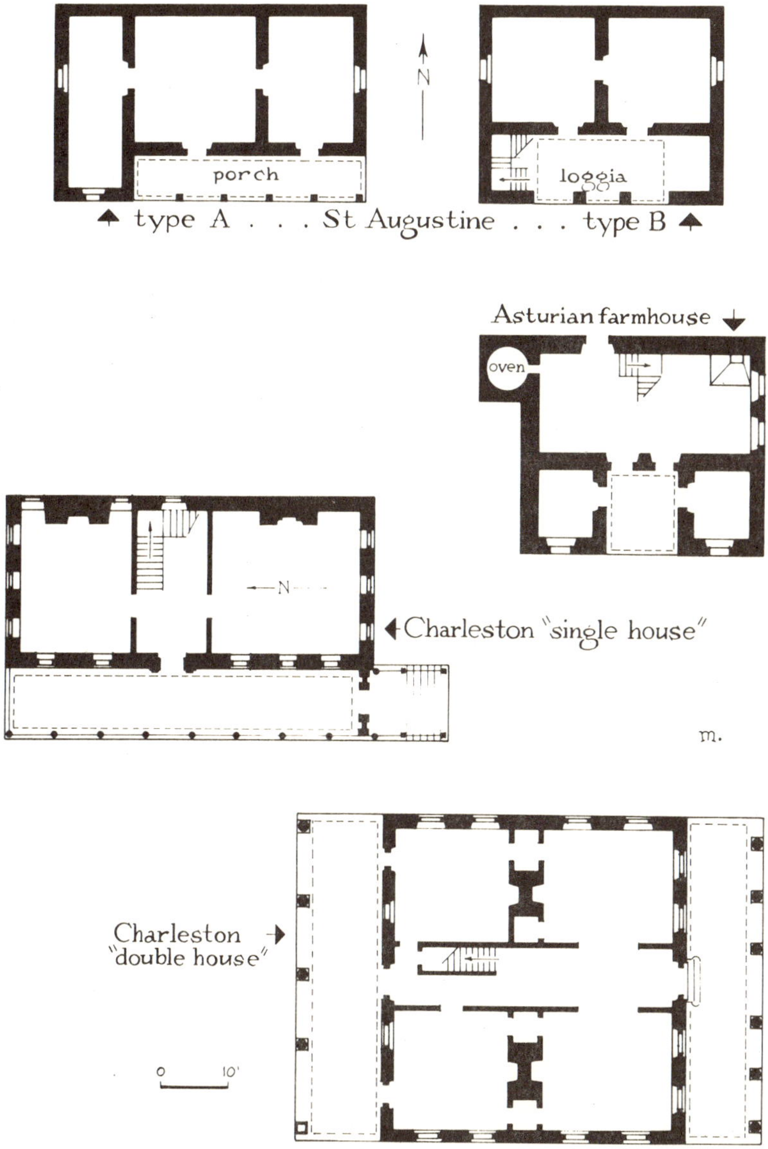

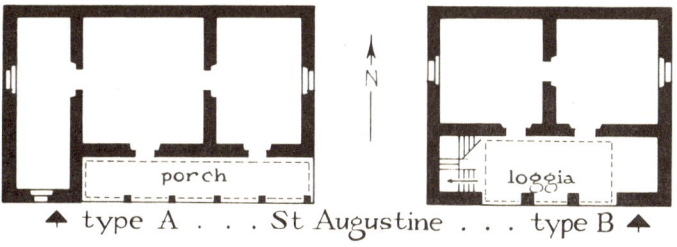

Fig. 3. Comparison of St. Augustine plan types (ground floors): Albert Manucy, *The Houses of St. Augustine*, pp. 55–57. Asturian: field observation and measurement of Casa Menéndez Suárez (Santa Apolonia, 65, Villalegre [Corvera], Oviedo province, Spain). Charleston single house: the Robert Pringle house (70 Tradd), after the first-floor plan in Albert Simons and Samuel Lapham, Jr., eds., *The Early Architecture of Charleston*, p. 52. Double house: the Horry house (59 Meeting), after the first-floor plan in Simons and Lapham, p. 52.

Taken together, these notes describe the entrance to a St. Augustine–plan house: a nine-foot-wide piazza or loggia, floored with lime concrete (Bartram called it "terrace") and the superstructure supported by posts or "Tuskan Pillars" (De Brahm's term for nonclassic stone columns) or an arcade. As the descriptions suggest, the St. Augustine plan does have alternate forms. The simpler one consists of two or more rooms fronted by a piazza, which is closed at one end by the body of house. Entrance is via the piazza, which faces the sideyard (never the street). If the house is two-story, the closed end of the piazza contains the stair. There may be a street balcony.

The more refined version of the plan has an open-sided room or loggia instead of a piazza.[8] In both cases, the plan is oriented to shield the piazza or loggia from north winds but to admit the low winter sunshine. In the summer the open area faces the prevailing southeast breeze, but gives shade from the burning sun overhead. Of 280 dwellings shown on the 1788 map, 60 have the St. Augustine plan with either loggia (32) or piazza (28). In view of the testimony by our three British observers, it is likely that most of the St. Augustine–plan houses were pre-British carry-overs, although during the English period at least one simple two-cell home was converted by stages into a two-story St. Augustine plan. Surely there must have been others.

In Asturias[9] I have seen ancient farmhouses with space disposed much like the St. Augustine plan, specifically with a loggia-like area facing south (see Fig. 3). The function of the open-sided room was clearly utilitarian: it housed the farm cart and sheltered the accesses to tool and supply storerooms, but there was nothing to prevent one from dozing here out of the wind in the winter sun or resting in its summer shade between chores. Is the Asturian plan a prototype of the St. Augustine plan? Quite possibly. At this stage of our research, however, the only evidence is similarity and the fact that Florida's colonists included many Asturians.[10]

8. As used here, the terms *piazza* and *loggia* are defined thus: Piazza—a roofed area along a façade, open on two or three sides, usually columned, sometimes arcaded; a porch. Loggia—a space contained within the body of a building and used as an open-air room, usually with the open side columned or arcaded.

9. Notably at Villalegre, a suburb of Avilés in Oviedo province, and at Treceño in Santander province.

10. Muster rolls in J. T. Connor, trans. and ed., *The Colonial Records of Florida, 1570–1580* (DeLand, Fla., 1925, 1930), 2:135–47, 163–69.

Perhaps austerity is the closest thing to a common denominator in Spain's tradition of vernacular architecture. It is, of course, supremely obvious in exterior façades. Not even the recklessly flowering plants of warm Andalucía can soften the spareness of the design, except in the delightful patios. For one reason or another the central patio (a descendent of the Roman atrium) did not take root in Florida, but other characteristics equally Spanish transplanted readily. The simple, unadorned street façade prevails yet. Other details—large windows shielded by gratings, balconies, arcades and galleries, and flat roofs—intrigued our British observers; Bartram noted "the best houses had large windows next the street, all bannistered and projecting a foot or more from the house wall . . . supported by a step of stone at the bottom. . . . Many bannisters of the back windows next to the yard or garden don't project out from the wall as the front windows, which often do a foot beyond the wall, so that it's very convenient sitting within the window, observing unseen what passeth in the street."[11] De Brahm added "The houses have to the East windows projecting 16 or 18 inches into the street, very wide and proportionately high."[12]

Door-size windows are found in many parts of Spain, but the out-jutting, on-street type is epitomized in the province of Cádiz, where the big openings encourage air circulation in the warm, dry climate.[13] A wrought-iron grating at each window is supported on a masonry step or corbel, and those who elect to sit in this projection enjoy a wide-angle view of the neighborhood along with exposure to any cooling breeze that happens along—all without loss of security or privacy. But in transportation from the Mother Country changes were inevitable. St. Augustine windows are relatively small in scale (though they seemed large to the English), and wood replaced the iron grating. Bartram wrote "[Some of] the inhabitants . . . built themselves good houses after the Spanish fashion, all or most with pleasant covered balconies, supported with double beams fastened in the wall . . ,"[14] while Stork described the houses as "commonly two stories high, with large windows and balconies."[15]

11. Bartram, *Diary of a Journey.*
12. De Brahm, "History of Three Provinces."
13. Personal observation.
14. Bartram, *Diary of a Journey.*
15. Stork, *A Description of East-Florida.*

108 / Eighteenth-Century Florida and the Revolution

Balconies are plentiful in Spain, but the long narrow type extending across the south elevation is perhaps most common in the northerly provinces, notably in the farmlands of the Asturians and Basques[16] (see Fig. 4). In this chilly, wet country, balconies are completely utilitarian. Built for drying grain and other farm produce, they are called *solanas*, sun galleries. Even in town their function is similar, with the family wash predominant on rainy days. In Florida the structural members of the balcony became shorter and heavier than the Spanish prototypes, perhaps because lumber was more plentiful, and the depth of the balcony increased from a narrow three or four feet to a comfortable five or six so there was room to sit in the breezy shade, keep an eye on the traffic below, or chat cozily with the neighbor sitting across the street on her balcony. "A row of pillars or arches generally supports a roof continuing from the common roof to the body of the house, if it be a shingled roof," wrote Bartram.[17]

Arcades and galleries are an integral part of the Spanish culture. They are especially conspicuous and welcome around the plazas, providing dry, sheltered walkways in all kinds of weather. Much less obvious are the private ones found inside the home, perhaps around a central patio, or facing the garden. These may range from rough posts supporting a crude wooden gallery over a little patio in a mud-built farmhouse near Burgos to elegant stone arches or columns adorning the tiled courtyard of a palace almost anywhere in Spain. Not much of architectural elegance came to Florida, but there were a few arches with proper capitals and moldings fronting the loggias, and more than a few piazza or gallery posts and columns. These are attested to not only by Bartram, but also by Dr. Stork, who wrote "before the entry of most of the houses runs a portico of stone arches," and William De Brahm, who said, "their entrances are shaded by Piazzas supported by Tuskan Pillars." De Brahm noted also that grape arbors amplified the entrance shade. The use of the deciduous vine in the dooryard is still common practice in Iberia, not to mention other Mediterranean lands.[18]

Bartram wrote that the "best houses is generally built of hewn shell stone, as is most of those that is flat roofed and terraced on the

16. Personal observation.
17. Bartram, *Diary of a Journey.*
18. Stork, *A Description of East-Florida*; De Brahm, "History of Three Provinces"; personal observation. Original arcades in various stages of preservation are found at 39, 143, and 214 St. George, 12 Avilés, 20 and 101 Charlotte.

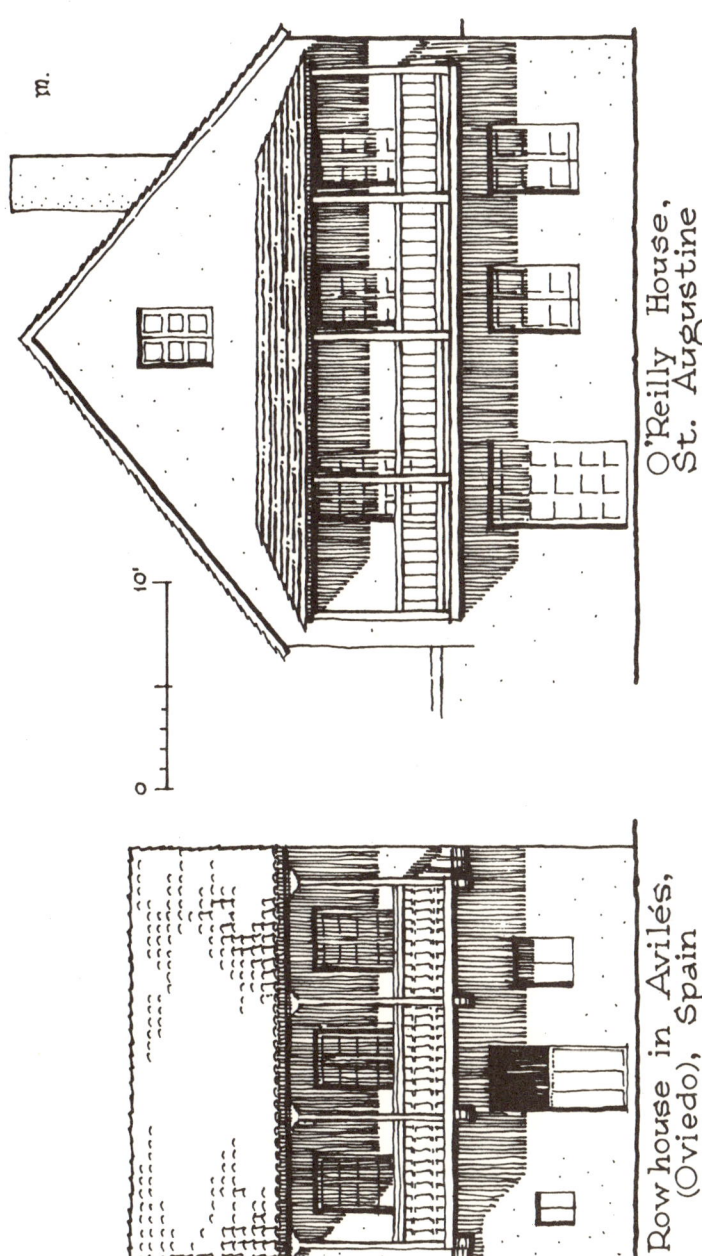

Fig. 4. Balconies. Row house: field observation and measurement of Casa Suárez Alvarez (Plaza de Carbayedo, 41, Avilés, Oviedo province, Spain). The O'Reilly house (32 Avilés), after Manucy, *Houses of St. Augustine*, p. 77.

ARCADE AT 44 AVENIDA MENÉNDEZ. This pre-1760 construction, characteristic of a St. Augustine plan, was not only the entrance to the house but a pleasant open-air room.

top, with stone battlements, which have pipes, mostly of burnt clay, let through the wall and projecting a foot or more to carry off the water."[19] Stork added "the roofs are commonly flat."[20] I must again point out that Bartram's "terrace" means a lime-concrete slab, and "best" houses were a minority. Bartram went on to say that most common houses had concrete walls ("lime-shell mortar mixed with sand, in which they pounded oyster shells as close as possible") with a palm-thatch roof, which was "very tight." Dr. Stork later qualified his "flat" statement with the notation that there were a lot of thatched roofs. As I mentioned earlier, a Spanish observer counted only twenty-three flat roofs in 1759!

Historically, flat roofs are found in arid lands; pitched roofs are for regions with rainfall. This generality, like all generalities, has notable exceptions: San Juan, Puerto Rico, has heavy rainfall but a multitude of flat roofs, while in the arid Virgin Islands the flat roofs are outnumbered by pitched roofs. Seemingly the steep-roof tradition of Denmark and England influenced Virgin Island construction, while flat-roof proponents from Spain built in Puerto Rico —and in St. Augustine. There is, of course, a much more compelling reason for flat roofs, and that is their resistance to fire. Spain's flat roofs are found almost entirely in the arid coastal provinces of Cádiz, Almería, and Alicante. They are of two types. The more primitive is a thick bed of clay over cane matting laid upon horizontal rafters. A top spread of gravel insulates and protects the clay surface.[21] The other roof is built-up masonry. Wooden slats, carefully positioned on the rafters, support a base layer of rectangular tiles. Over the first tiles, a second layer is bedded in lime mortar, thus completing a substantial slab about three inches thick.

At St. Augustine, scarcity of clay and abundance of rain proscribed the first type. Of the second type, there was one known example (44 St. George Street), but nothing extant. In fact, the only flat roof left is at Castillo de San Marcos, which is not exactly vernacular housing. Our best guess on flat roofs in Florida, therefore, is that most of them consisted of a dense lime-concrete slab over board sheathing.[22]

19. Bartram, *Diary of a Journey*.
20. Stork, *A Description of East-Florida*.
21. Personal observation.
22. For more detailed discussion, see Manucy, *Houses of St. Augustine*, pp. 104–8.

ENGLISH TRADITION

In the review which follows I stress English practice in South Carolina and Georgia, for from these two colonies came most of the loyalists who flocked to Florida after the onset of the American Revolution. Charleston (1670) began with a "Grand Modell" plan, which included a central square at the intersection of its two "Great Streets." The square as such no longer exists, but its function as a public-use area remains since public buildings are on three of the corners and a church adorns the fourth. Charleston's growth, however, seems to have been influenced less by schematicism than by natural compromises between private and public interests. For example, a 1739 map bisects the town square with a community-encircling line of fortifications. The other emphasis was clearly upon the commodious waterfront where a number of public buildings were built: markets, the council chamber and guardhouse, the customshouse, the courthouse and the exchange. The allotted space on the waterfront was, if not ample, seemingly sufficient for these community structures.[23]

By the latter part of the seventeenth and during the eighteenth centuries, English settlement planning did not differ markedly from earlier Spanish specifications. Savannah (1733) and Frederica (1736) were both laid out with rectangular street grids, beyond which were commons, garden plots, and farm acreage (fifty acres for each freeholder). Additionally, Savannah's plan contained a system of small squares intersecting the street grid. Certain lots around each square, as with the Spanish plaza, were intended for public buildings. Today the little green parks are a pleasant remnant of Savannah's past.[24]

23. A facsimile of the "Grand Modell" is reproduced in Alice R. Huger Smith and D. E. Huger Smith, *The Dwelling Houses of Charleston, South Carolina* (New York, 1917), p. 22; the 1739 facsimile, "The Ichnography of Charles-Town at High Water," is on p. 21. A clearer reproduction of the latter is in Albert Simons and Samuel Lapham, Jr., eds., *The Early Architecture of Charleston* (Columbia, 1970).

24. Peter Gordon, *View of Savannah*, 1734, in the library of the Georgia Historical Society, Savannah; Mills Lane, *Savannah Revisited: A Pictorial History* (Savannah, 2d. ed., 1973), p. 14: "A Map of the County of Savannah" (1741), and p. 24: Thomas Shruder, "Plat of Savannah" (1770); [Samuel Augspourguer], "A Plan of Fredericka a Town in the Plantation of Georgia . . . 1736," is in the John Carter Brown Library, Brown University, photocopy at Fort Frederica National Monument, St. Simons Island, Georgia; Margaret

Changing Traditions in St. Augustine Architecture / 113

The Georgia freeholder was obliged, in return for his grant of land, to build on his town lot a substantial house, at least sixteen by twenty-four feet in size, with eight-foot headroom. Founder James Oglethorpe ordered two such houses from Carolina, an act which suggests that the type was also the standard minimum house in Carolina. In any case, they must have served as models for his artisan colonists who had just come from England. The sixteen-by-twenty-four-foot dimensions had evolved from the ancient unit of space needed to stable an oxen team and underlines the extent to which medievalism still permeated English building practice.[25]

A few of Savannah's little frame dwellings are preserved photographically. Charleston has kept a handful of early-eighteenth-century houses. One of these, the tall narrow row house at 17 Chalmers, with a one-room-upon-a-floor plan, tiny windows and a steep tile roof, is clearly in the medieval tradition. So are certain small, cramped, and irregular floor plans found at the Frederica site—an archeological time capsule for the decade following 1736. Other Frederica foundations, however, show roomy and symmetrical plans which are surely evidence of the transition then taking place in English architecture.[26]

For despite the persistence of medievalism, changes were under way in the Mother Country by the late 1600s. In small-house construction, lean-tos and outshuts and dormers gave the family more room; "guillotine," or sash, windows came into fashion, and gambrel or hip roofs replaced the steep gables. The transition led to a roomier, more formal style which came to maturity during the reigns of the Georges from whom it took its name. Georgian archi-

---

Davis Cate, "Fort Frederica," *Georgia Historical Quarterly* 27 (June 1943): 114, 118.

25. C. C. Jones, Jr., *History of Georgia* (Boston, 1883), 1:156–60, quoting a deed of December 21, 1733, then in the office of the Georgia Secretary of State; *Collections of the Georgia Historical Society* (Savannah, 1840–1916), 1:23; Frederick D. Nichols, *The Early Architecture of Georgia* (Chapel Hill, N.C., 1957), pp. 18, 26, 27; Sidney R. Jones, *English Village Homes* (London, 1947), pp. 88–89.

26. Lane, *Savannah Revisited*, pp. 40–43; Evangeline Davis and N. Jane Iseley, *Charleston Houses and Gardens* (Charleston, 1975); Simons and Lapham, *Early Architecture*, especially pp. 30, 80; Charles H. Fairbanks, J. W. Moore, Jr., and Joel L. Shiner: various reports on archeological excavations at Frederica (National Park Service, 1947–53, 1958–59); these data are synthesized in Albert Manucy, "Specifications for a Scale Model of the Town of Frederica in Georgia about 1742" (National Park Service, 1960), Fort Frederica National Monument files.

tecture meant symmetry, rather than irregularity, spaciousness rather than closeness, and in the better structures, decoration with elements of the classic orders. Visually the results were simple rectangular masses with double files of rooms, level cornice lines and hip roofs, uniform ranges of classic windows, and frame and pedimented doorways. The new style was brought to the colonies by builders emigrating from England and, perhaps more important, between the covers of handbooks containing designs and details for builders and prospective homeowners.[27]

Charleston's Robert Brewton house (71 Church), built before 1733, is one of the earliest Georgian buildings in the colonies. Because it has only a single file rather than a double file of rooms, this manifestation of the Georgian style is known in Charleston as a "single house" (see Fig. 3). It exemplifies intelligent adaptation of a house plan to the local environment—in this case, a temperate coastal climate. Being but one room in depth, the single house had maximum cross ventilation. The building was oriented with the short side on the street. The long side, with entrance to a central stair hall, faced south or southwest on the sideyard (as did many of the Spanish houses in St. Augustine). Piazzas along this side were added. An "English" basement, that is, a basement partly above ground, plus the high-ceilinged stories above, raised the building within reach of the summer breezes from the sea. The Robert Brewton house was one of the first to achieve three stories, but this height was not uncommon thereafter. Since the basement elevated the ground floor as much as five feet above grade and eighteenth-century ceilings were about ten feet for the lower story, nine to twelve for the second, and eight to ten for the third, the prominence of a fine house was impressive, even with the relatively low roof lines of the new vogue.[28]

Charleston's "double house" is quite typically Georgian in plan, with a double file of rooms, center hall, and entrance directly from

27. Informative discussions of the architectural transitions and manifestations are found in Harry Batsford and Charles Fry, *The English Cottage* (London, 1950), pp. 16–18; Henry C. Forman, *Architecture of the Old South* (Cambridge, Mass., 1948), pp. 5, 90–103; Sidney R. Jones, *English Village Homes*, pp. 88ff.; Fiske Kimball, *Domestic Architecture of the American Colonies and of the Early Republic* (New York, 1966), pp. 53–55, 58.

28. Samuel G. Stoney, *This Is Charleston. A Survey of the Architectural Heritage* . . . (Charleston, 1944), p. 25; Simons and Lapham, *Early Architecture*, pp. 22–23, 30, 52; Smith and Smith, *Dwelling Houses of Charleston*, pp. 43–45; Kimball, *Domestic Architecture*, pp. 72, 81–83.

Changing Traditions in St. Augustine Architecture / 115

the street (see Fig. 3). It is exemplified in the pre-Revolutionary Miles Brewton house (27 King), the design of which apparently owes much to Andrea Palladio, the noted sixteenth-century Italian architect whose architectural folios deeply influenced eighteenth-century England.[29]

Pre-Revolutionary Charleston was not all fine homes, of course, any more than Savannah was all one- or two-cell houses. But the examples I have cited show major aspects of the English tradition in the colonies that supplied much of St. Augustine's population in the years after 1775.

ENGLISH ST. AUGUSTINE (1764–84)

St. Augustine habitations in the mid-eighteenth century occupied an area about 0.7 mile long and less than 0.2 mile wide on the western shore of Matanzas Bay. Castillo de San Marcos, at the northeast corner of the settlement, had fair command of the harbor entrance as well as of the land approach from the north. All sides of the town were protected by adjacent water and marsh, military works, or both.[30]

Central in the town was the plaza. And facing the plaza on the west was the largest and most elaborate residence, the governor's house. A contemporary sketch represents it with a two-story gabled façade containing a street door beneath a massive covered balcony on corbeled supports. The fence wall along the street is integrated with the façade; one section is raised all the way to the eave of the house and is crowned with a cornice and balustrade. The cornice is supported visually by four engaged Doric columns on elevated bases, paired on each side of a tall gate into the courtyard, with gardens and outbuildings beyond. Looming west of the residence is a square, castellated tower. The English made few changes to the property beyond heightening the tower and building a stable, coach house, and laundry.[31]

29. Stoney, *This Is Charleston*, p. 29; Simons and Lapham, *Early Architecture*, pp. 36–50; Smith and Smith, *Dwelling Houses of Charleston*, pp. 50–52; Kimball, *Domesitc Architecture*, pp. 96–101; Banister Fletcher, *A History of Architecture on the Comparative Method* (London, 1931), pp. 654, 659.

30. Pablo Castelló, "Plano del Presidio de San Agustín de la Florida . . . [1764]," Ministry of War MSS 9–1–51(1), Madrid, reproduced in Chatelain, *Defenses of Spanish Florida*, Map 13.

31. "View of the Governors house at St. Augustine in E. Florida, Novr. 1764" (British Museum watercolor), reproduced in Archer B. Hulbert, *Crown*

116 / Eighteenth-Century Florida and the Revolution

At the east end of the plaza was the guardhouse, a functional one-story masonry structure with castellations to give it a military aspect.[32] This too underwent no major change. On the south line was a residence intended by the Spanish for the auxiliary bishop. The English, desperate for troop housing, lodged seventy men here. Not long afterward the governor remodeled it into a statehouse containing the offices of customs, land survey, secretary, and navy.[33]

A few yards farther south was the military hospital, but the English did not care for this central location and moved the facility to a Spanish-built church in an Indian village just north of the town. The former hospital became courthouse and jail.[34]

Also south of the plaza was another church, now used by the Anglicans. Renovation added a fine bell-and-clock tower in the contemporary style (see Fig. 5). An elevation of this tower is one of the very few surviving sketches of English civil construction during the period. Unfortunately, the draftsman omitted the church itself.[35]

When the Spaniards departed, they left real estate titles in the hands of their agent, one Jesse Fish, an Englishman with New York commercial connections who had lived at St. Augustine since the 1730s. There were almost 350 houses, all masonry except about 80. However, better than half of the masonry was tabby with wood framing, highly vulnerable to soldiers foraging for firewood.[36]

The problem of lodgings for the military was not properly solved until 1771. By then the Spanish monastery of St. Francis had been

---

Collection . . . of American Maps, Series II (Cleveland, 1910), vol. 1, no. 32. For British innovations here and elsewhere in the town, see Charles L. Mowat, "St. Augustine under the British Flag," *Florida Historical Quarterly* 20 (1941): 131–50.

32. "View from the Governors Window in St. Augustine E. Florida, Novr. 1764" (British Museum watercolor), reproduced in Hulbert, *Crown Collection*, no. 33.

33. Ricardo Torres-Reyes, *British Garrison of St. Augustine 1763–1784* (National Park Service, 1972), pp. 47–49.

34. Ibid., pp. 47, 55. A plan of the courthouse is in Colonial Office Papers 5/551–50, Public Record Office (London), and photocopies are in the libraries of the St. Augustine Historical Society and Historic St. Augustine Preservation Board.

35. Elevation of steeple for St. Peters Church, St. Augustine, Florida, Colonial Office Papers 5/554–3. Photocopies are in the libraries cited in note 34.

36. Manucy, *Houses of St. Augustine*, p. 33. For exposition of Fish's involvement in property transfers, see Robert L. Gold, *Borderland Empires in Transition: The Triple-Nation Transfer of Florida* (Carbondale, Ill., 1969).

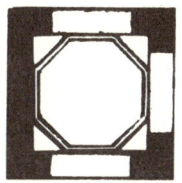

Fig. 5. Steeple of St. Peters, St. Augustine. Reproduction of photocopy from Colonial Office Papers 5/554-3 (Public Record Office, London). Date of the drawing is 1772.

HEADQUARTERS, FLORIDA DEPARTMENT OF MILITARY AFFAIRS, MARINE STREET AT ST. FRANCIS. Originally a Franciscan monastery (ca. 1730), the structure was converted to a barracks by the British just before the American Revolution.

Changing Traditions in St. Augustine Architecture / 119

converted into quarters, and commodious new barracks built. The barracks, prefabricated in New York, comprised a three-story, E-shaped frame structure with porches round about and topped by a cupola and a weathercock. The monastery, where British officers now meditated in the austere cells, was a large but unpretentious stone building standing near the southern limit of the town. It is still used by the military.[37]

But until these barracks, many soldiers had to make do as best they could. Some of the married ones moved into old huts or built new ones. Others took over empty, half-ruined hovels and existed there with neither beds nor bedding. Some died from exposure or from too much rum, their handiest weapon against the cold.[38] The unfortunate situation caused the loss of dozens of unoccupied humble dwellings which, as Bartram put it, "was built by the common [Spanish] soldiers and poor people at different times, as they could get money to enlarge them, the new and old walls is apt to wind and crack so that the [English] soldiers can easily pull them to pieces for their wood to burn, which is scarce here."[39] According to the naturalist, the soldiers pulled down "above half the town," leaving it in "a very ruinous condition." But, he added, "most of the best houses stand yet, several of them altered by the English. . . . The sun and light now begins to shine through glass and many chimneys is peeping above the roofs of the houses."[40] Actually, chimneys and glazed windows, though rare, had been present in pre-British St. Augustine.

Alterations were by no means confined to hearths and windows. Other examples: Benjamin Lord, surveyor general for East Florida, bought a lot with an old Spanish house and an outbuilding. He plastered the house walls, mended the roof, glazed the windows and painted. The outbuilding became a kitchen combined with a store and shed. John Moore, victualler and innkeeper, bought a Spanish house which had a shingle roof but no floor, and a detached, flat-roofed kitchen. John enlarged the house to seven rooms and "a Garret fit for an assembly." All was floored, plastered, and whitewashed. He built a new frame kitchen and put a store into the

37. Charles L. Mowat, "St. Francis Barracks, St. Augustine: A Link with the British Regime," *Florida Historical Quarterly* 21 (1943):266–80.
38. Torres-Reyes, *British Garrison*, pp. 47–50.
39. Bartram, *Diary of a Journey*.
40. Ibid.

120 / Eighteenth-Century Florida and the Revolution

old one. Later he bought more land and built another inn, six rooms, two-story with a balcony, privies, and a five-horse stable.[41] These were but a few of the changes that came as émigrés from the colonies swarmed in toward the end of the Revolution. St. Augustine's population swelled to nearly three thousand people. Many of the new people had to leave valuable property behind. Such a one was Colonel John Stuart, who, as superintendent of Indian affairs for the southern district, allegedly encouraged Britain's red allies to collect patriot scalps. Stuart fled Charleston, leaving a fine new house (ca. 1772), built at a reputed cost of £18,000, to be confiscated by the patriot authorities.[42]

It does not appear that Stuart or any other had such elaborate homes in St. Augustine. A few had dismantled their modest houses and brought them along, as did William Curtis, a shopkeeper, in 1782. He sold this house, complete with doors, sashes, and shutters, and built himself a new one. For others the only shelters were a new generation of thatch huts, hastily built and later replaced by little timberframe houses. What were these frame houses like? Only one example of an antique timberframe house (14 St. George) is extant at St. Augustine (see Fig. 6). Its construction date is uncertain, but the basic dimensions (about eighteen by twenty-three feet) along with the catslide roof and the method of framing are in the tradition of the minimum house specified for the Colony of Georgia by its trustees during an earlier time.[43]

A goodly number of the new citizens were self-reliant tradesmen. Robert Robinson, a butcher who made extensive repairs and alterations to his property, stated that "the Work was Chiefly done by him and a Negroe of his own, but that he sometimes hired a Negroe Carpenter." Those who had slaves trained for construction work certainly used them or hired them out to others. There were white artisans as well, such as James Scotland, carpenter, Davis Yeats, a tiler, and John Tully, a "stone builder" (mason).

And there was William Watson, called a house carpenter. Watson was a mature journeyman who came to Florida from England in

41. Manucy, *Houses of St. Augustine*, pp. 34–40, 98, 155.
42. Smith and Smith, *Dwelling Houses of Charleston*, pp. 239–47; J. Leitch Wright, Jr., *British St. Augustine* (St. Augustine, 1975), p. 45.
43. Manucy, *Houses of St. Augustine*, pp. 36, 60; J. Leitch Wright, Jr., *Florida in the American Revolution* (Gainesville, Fla., 1975), p. 126; Lane, *Savannah Revisited*, pp. 40–44; personal observation.

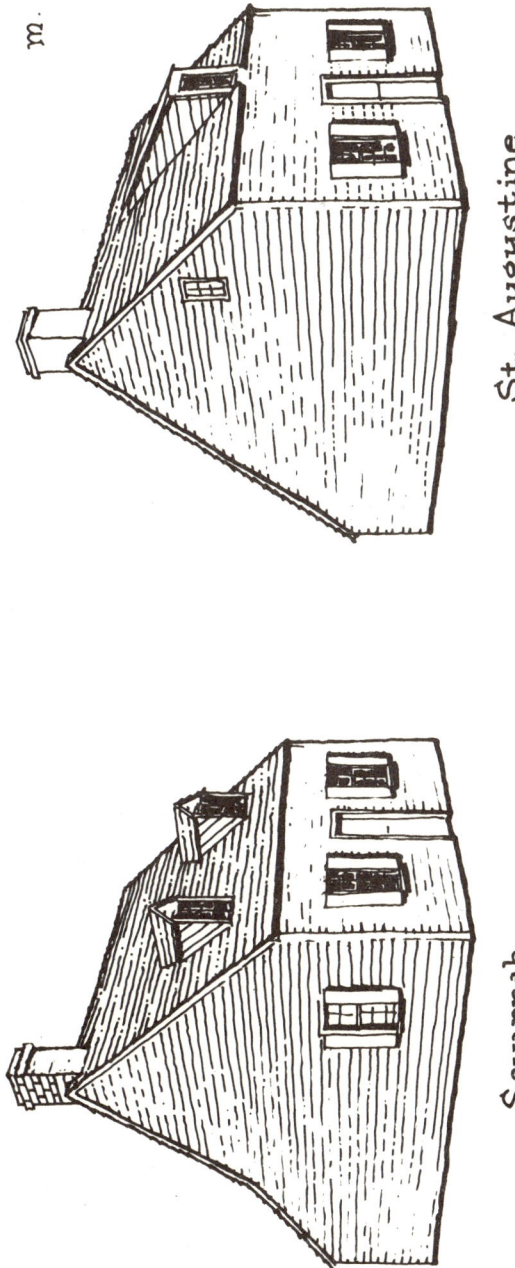

Fig. 6. Timberframes. Savannah: the cottage of Christian Camphor (122 East Oglethorpe), built ca. 1760. The sketch is after the photograph in Mills Lane, *Savannah Revisited*, p. 41. St. Augustine: the Gianopoli house (14 St. George).

14 ST. GEORGE STREET. Time has nudged its frame askew, but this St. Augustine cottage has the look of the "minimum house" prescribed for Georgia settlers in the 1730s. Seemingly its style is one of the "new" traditions brought to Spanish Florida by loyalist immigrants.

AGUILAR-SEGUÍ HOUSE, 224 ST. GEORGE STREET. Archeologists date the first floor from the 1770s. The frame story was added two generations later. A felicitous blend of uncluttered plan and Anglo-Spanish - American traditions produced this straightforward, eminently livable home of Mr. and Mrs. William King Moeller.

124 / Eighteenth-Century Florida and the Revolution

1766 and stayed until after the change in sovereignty. He bought and renovated old houses or built new ones and sold them all for profit. He must have been a man with better than average imagination, for he is credited with having converted a twenty-by-eighty-foot range of stables into a proper dwelling. Not only did he own £25 of "Books of Architecture & others," but he had a large tract up North River from which twenty blacks kept him supplied with lumber and shingles.

Unluckily, after Will left St. Augustine, a shipwreck cost him all his books, tools, and other gear. He and his wife found themselves back in London, grown old, and faced with making a new start in life. And so it was with others, for with the peace of 1783 the majority of British citizens followed their flag out of Florida. The building boom was over.[44]

THE "PEOPLE-MIX" PERIOD (1784–1800)

St. Augustine would never again be a truly Spanish town. Most of the hundred or so Spanish-speaking citizens who came after Florida's retrocession to Spain were either native-born Floridians or Canary Islanders. The largest population segment was the 450 colonists who comprised the remnant of those recruited from the Mediterranean for Turnbull's New Smyrna plantation. They had resettled at St. Augustine in 1777. About 300 Britons had also decided to stay on, and there were some 500 blacks in the province, a good many of them living in town. Negro, Britisher, Minorcan, Greek, Italian, Spaniard, Canary Islander and *Floridano*—this was a diverse population indeed.[45]

But in 1784, it was not a prosperous community. Forty percent of the houses (110 of 277) were rated uninhabitable by the government engineer.[46] Still, the better houses soon had tenants and a traveler wrote that the cottages of the Minorcans "in the narrow streets nearest the water, were . . . picturesque; festooned with nets and roses, shaded by orange trees; and hung round with cages of

44. Manucy, *Houses of St. Augustine*, pp. 37, 41.
45. Ibid, p. 43.
46. Mariano de la Rocque, "Noticia del estado en que se hallan las Casas de la Ciudad de Sn. Agustín de la Florida," St. Augustine, Oct. 11, 1784. With his map of the same date, "Plano de la Ciudad de San Agustín de la Florida," MS. tracing, library of Castillo de San Marcos National Monument, St. Augustine.

XIMÉNEZ-FATIO HOUSE, 20 AVILÉS STREET. Built in 1798, it typifies the St. Augustine style as it was toward the end of Florida's colonial period.

126 / Eighteenth-Century Florida and the Revolution

nonpareils and other singing birds"[47]—a description which suggests a not unpleasant style of living.

A number of houses from the late 1700s and early 1800s have survived. They range from small to large and from traditional to "modern," because the owners themselves were of various classes and backgrounds, including government official, planter, merchant, fisherman, farmer, artisan, and soldier.

In many ways the most representative house of this era is the Ximénex-Fatio house (1798) at 20 Avilés, which is now the property of the National Society of the Colonial Dames of America in the State of Florida (see Fig. 7). It is a two-story, shellstone structure with street balcony, dormered garret, steep hip roof, and detached kitchen. Rooms are high ceilinged and spacious in the Georgian tradition. The floor plan is basically St. Augustine, with the conventional off-street entrance and stairway in the loggia on the yard. There is also, however, a central entrance in the street façade, a characteristic of many new houses of the time, probably traceable to English tradition. Long and varied commercial use of the building (Ximénez himself was a merchant) accounts for other doors that were punched through exterior walls.[48]

The Spanish government was responsible for military and other administration-related construction. The architect for such projects during this period was the royal engineer of the province, Mariano de la Rocque. The new portal he designed in 1785 for the chapel at the Castillo documents his training in the precepts of neoclassicism. He framed its round-arched doorway with pilasters supporting a classic entablature and, by judicious use of tile-red plaster on the finials and other decorative elements, stressed its centrality in a long white façade.[49]

De la Rocque was also architect for the parish church (1797), now the Cathedral of St. Augustine. Here he combined a curved gable (familiar to us in so-called mission architecture), Doric columns, and a broken pediment to achieve a simple, effective

47. Charles J. Latrobe, *The Rambler in North America, 1832–1833* (New York, 1835), pp. 35–36.
48. National Society of the Colonial Dames of America in the State of Florida, *Turn Left at the Plaza* (1976), Tour 1, Item 2.
49. Graphic recapitulation of Rocque's sketches for the chapel door: "Vista de la puerta de la capilla de Sn. Marcos de Sn. Augustín de la Florida, tomada de las borradores del proyecto de 12 de mayo de 1785, firmado por Mariano de la Rocque," April 15, 1891, copy (from Havana archives) in Castillo library.

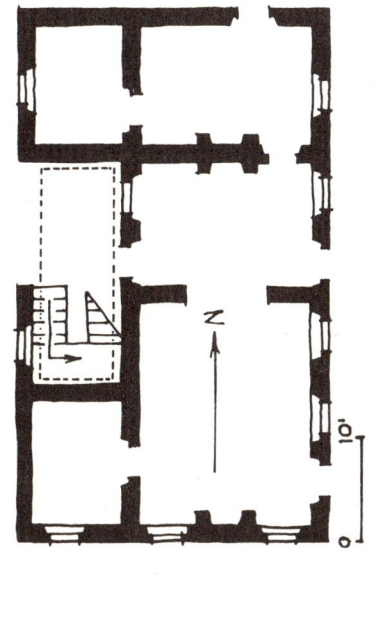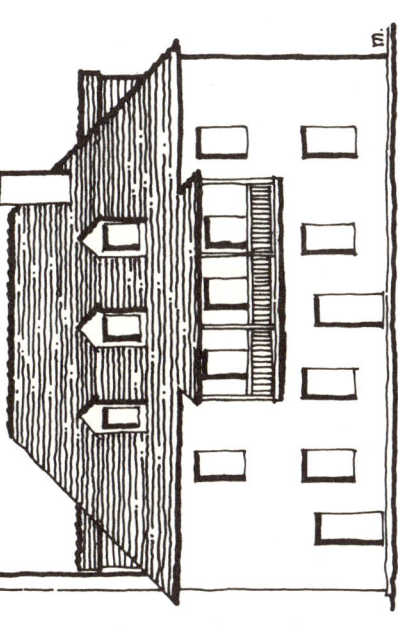

Fig. 7. Ximénez-Fatio house. After Manucy, *Houses of St. Augustine*, p. 60 (Fig. 27) and p. 78 (Fig. 35W).

façade of excellent scale. Bells mounted in the high gable were rung from a hidden gallery behind the façade, above the nave roof. The nave was rectangular, 41 by 124 feet, with shellstone walls 25 inches thick reinforced by pilasters to the full 25-foot height. The stability of this engineer-designed wall was proven in 1887, when only the four walls, along with the adornments of the street façade, survived a fire which destroyed the entire neighborhood.[50]

In addition to architecture of the late 1700s and early 1800s, a number of pre-1760 houses still exist. All of them have undergone major remodellings to accommodate the different cultures and lifestyles of successive inhabitants. The changes recorded in the fabric of each building give deeper perspective to our comprehension of the Anglo-Spanish-American influences.

Several of these structures have been studied intensively, combining the disciplines of historian, archeologist, and architect. Some of the sites were occupied in the seventeenth century or before, but of that era only structural rudiments and artifacts remain. Yet enough remains to establish the pattern. The Arrivas house (44 St. George) began as a one-cell tabby house. It was destroyed during the English siege of 1702. It was replaced some years later with a two-room stone structure with porch, later modified to a three-room St. Augustine plan. A frame second story was added in the late eighteenth century, and there was further renovation and alteration about 1830, the period to which the building has been restored by the Historic St. Augustine Preservation Board.[51]

Across the street, the Avero house (39 St. George) was, in the early eighteenth century, a two-cell tabby house. It was replaced before 1743 by a stone building of St. Augustine plan, which has come through numerous alterations surprisingly intact. The Llambías house (31 St. Francis) began as a one-story stone building; it was later enlarged to a two-story St. Augustine plan with a balcony. The royal treasurer's house (143 St. George) was a one-story, U-shaped plan with a patio arcade when it was built, but lost a wing and gained a second story in the 1830s.[52]

50. Jane Quinn, *Minorcans in Florida* (St. Augustine, 1975), pp. 97–98, 100, 110–12.
51. Lane, *Houses of St. Augustine*, p. 24; Historic St. Augustine Preservation Board, *Guidebook* (1971), pp. 25–26.
52. Kathleen A. Deagan, "Report on the Archeological Investigation of SA–13–5 (The Avero House) St. Augustine, Florida" (Florida State University, 1974), 1, Architectural Data; Stuart Barnette, "The Restoration of the

GONZÁLEZ - PEAVETT - ALVAREZ HOUSE, 14 ST. FRANCIS STREET, as seen from the museum arcade of the St. Augustine Historical Society. This seldom photographed off-street façade has the austere aspect of a farmhouse in Spain.

The house with the earliest documentation is the St. Augustine Historical Society's Oldest House (14 St. Francis), more formally called the González-Peavett-Alvarez house (see Fig. 8). Archeological relationships of artifacts and floor levels, plus structural evidence and historical records, define distinct stages in the evolution of the site. Briefly, they are as follows:

Seventeenth century.—Human occupation from the early 1600s, with loss of a dwelling by fire about 1700. This was doubtless the holocaust of 1702.

1727.—A two-room masonry house with a corner hearth was built sometime between 1703 and 1727. Owner: Tomás González Hernández, Spanish soldier.

1775.—After 1775 a timberframe second story, hip roof, and another hearth were added. Owner: Major Joseph Peavett, English soldier.

1788.—Before 1788 another file of rooms was added on the north and a porch on the east. Owners: Peavett to 1786; Mary, his widow, to 1790; Gerónimo Alvarez, Spanish baker and politician, and his heirs to 1882.

Nineteenth century.—In 1886, a round tower was added for the dentist-owner's office. Owners: William Duke to 1884; Dr. C. P. Carver to 1898.

Twentieth century.—About 1907 an apartment was added on the west side, along with a garage for "Red Devil," a horseless carriage. In 1959–60, the St. Augustine Historical Society removed the post-1800 additions and accomplished other restorative work. Owners: J. W. Henderson to 1911; George Reddington et al. to 1918; St. Augustine Historical Society.[53]

Thus did the dwelling change, adding features one by one with the changing times. It grew from a simple single-story shelter to an early twentieth-century "modern," complete with dental chair and attached garage apartment. Yet there was a constant reminder of its ancient origin: the ground floor ceiling seemingly came ever lower as street and floor levels were built up during the decades, and as human generations grew taller.

Llambias House" (St. Augustine, 1954), library of the St. Augustine Historical Society. For investigations at the Treasurer's House, see reports in the files of the Historic St. Augustine Preservation Board, and Lane, *Houses of St. Augustine*, pp. 58–59, 90–91, 108, 113.

53. Frederik C. Gjessing et al., *Evolution of the Oldest House* (Tallahassee, 1962), vol. 7 of *Notes in Anthropology*. See especially chaps. 3–5.

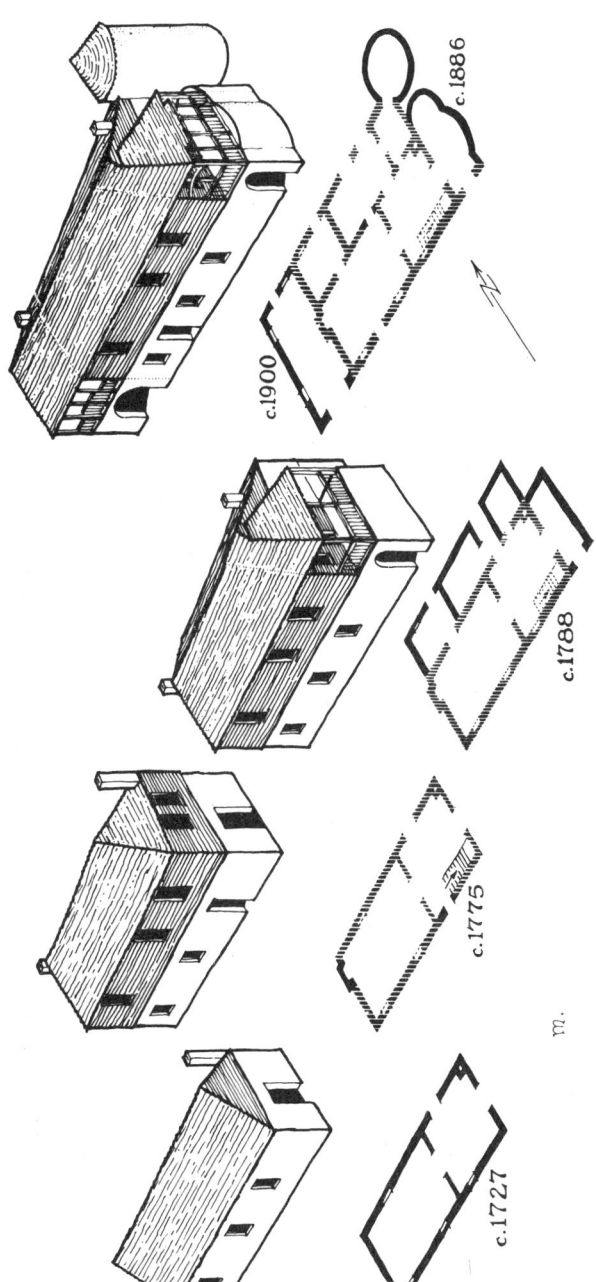

Fig. 8. González–Peavett–Alvarez house. After Gjessing's architectural sketches, as modified by later historical and archeological findings, in Frederik Gjessing et al., *Evolution of the Oldest House*.

The confrontation between Spanish and English architectural traditions in the little Florida town melded into a new tradition that was neither Spanish nor English, but St. Augustinian.

The Spanish foundation had remarkable solidity, comprising as it did the inflexible old town plan with its narrow shaded streets. Upon this foundation the Spanish builders erected simple, utilitarian houses which were well adapted to the environment. But neither of the great traditions, as they met at St. Augustine, was purely Spanish or purely English, for the transplantings from the homelands had flowered diversely as they grew in the American climates. What the English inherited at St. Augustine was vernacular architecture, and the features they added were in a vernacular of their own. Nor should we forget that their influence did not leave St. Augustine after the twenty allotted years; many British chose to stay after their flag had gone, and they were joined in later years by Americans—other erstwhile Britons—who also opted for a Florida future.

The houses which have survived are massive masonry buildings, cool in summer, warm in winter, sound and practical, and not to be changed in a hurry. Yet, as we have seen, radical adjustments could be made to meet new conditions, and indeed often were. It was not unusual to double the size of a small masonry home by adding a timberframe story; flat roofs gave way to shingled gable or hip roofs, often with dormers in the garret. And while the trend was unmistakably toward high-ceilinged spaciousness in the Georgian manner, even the new houses kept such niceties as loggias and street balconies, which were not only functional but pleasing to the eye and comfortable for living. Economics never permitted the architectural opulence found in Charleston, and in St. Augustine the qualities of extreme simplicity and utility were never lost.

British Material Culture

in St. Augustine:

The Artifact as Social Commentary

THOMAS G. LEDFORD

THE bicentennial anniversary of the American Revolution has caused scholars and citizens to pause and wonder what our country was like two hundred years ago. Florida was a British colony not unlike the thirteen who rebelled, but there were differences, and these differences have intrigued students of history for many decades. Florida's deep prehistoric traditions, her rich Hispanic heritage, her loyalty to Great Britain, and her role in the growth of the United States have lured scholars to delve into her past and peel away the patina of antiquity to reveal the facets of her life. But what about East Florida, the British colony, and St. Augustine, the center stage in a twenty-year drama under the Union flag? Historians have provided the actors and the scenes of this play, but what of the scenery, the props, or the costumes? Until recently archeologists have concentrated on other areas of interest, the aboriginal natives of the state, the Spanish dominion, or the American Period, but now attention is being drawn to the twenty-year segment when Florida was a British colony among many others.

In 1974, a well, which had been built by the Spaniards soon after Governor James Moore's attack of 1702, was discovered in the plaza of St. Augustine. The well had remained in use until about 1784 when the British filled it with debris from trash pits in the plaza and abandoned it. The well provides us with a time capsule, a small inventory of British material culture typical of the 1763–84 era.

Ceramics play a key role in an archeologist's interpretation of historic sites, and British ceramics are perhaps the best-known and most thoroughly understood aspect of this cultural horizon. They provide a key not only to the chronological position of a site but to aspects of culture including economic and social status and trade. The plaza well was filled with British ceramics of types which are closely associated with British culture in the eighteenth century. Creamware is a refined earthenware, perfected by Josiah Wedgewood by 1762, having a yellowish-white finish resembling porcelain.[1] It was in fact an imitation of oriental porcelain produced in England to compete in the world market. Forty-seven percent of the sherds recovered from the well are of this type. It graced the table of the English royal family and certainly appeared on genteel tables in St. Augustine and in the plantation houses along the St. Johns River. Oriental porcelain, so popular and influential in Europe during the eighteenth century, comprised 11 percent of the ceramics from this site. It, too, was expensive and indicated the presence of a social elite.

The ever present Spanish olive jar, indicative of the worldwide trade network, made up 10 percent of all ceramics recovered. Its occurrence is not surprising in a British site, nor does it compromise the contents of the well. Olive jars are found as far away as Cape Breton Island, Nova Scotia, and southward along the Atlantic Coast as well as in East Florida.[2] They do not necessarily indicate direct trade with Spain, but they may have originated in a northern colony involved in the properous coastal trade. English slipware, white saltglazed sherds, and tin enameled delft were also recovered from the well, indicating their presence in the colony. They are not nearly so numerous as the more fashionable styles, but combined with the other types found in the well, form a complex of materials indicative of British culture in the second half of the eighteenth century.

Glass outnumbers other artifactual material from the well by a large margin. Green types associated with spirit containers are predominant, and while the eighteenth century is well known for its enjoyment of alcoholic beverages, paint, oil, medicine, and a variety of other liquids were also held in these vessels. Clear glass was more expensive to produce, and its use was generally confined to

1. Ivor Noel-Hume, *A Guide to Artifacts of Colonial America* (New York, 1969), p. 125.
2. Charles H. Fairbanks, "Spanish Artifacts at the Fortress of Louisbourg, Cape Breton Island," *The Conference on Historic Site Archaeology Papers* (1974), 9:32–33.

window panes, drinking glasses, decanters, and ornamental pieces. Several wine glass stems were recovered showing the delicate white ribbon twist popular from 1755 to 1775.[3] Such glasses would enrich any eighteenth-century table. A cut-glass inkwell or sand bottle with a pewter top came out of the mud and might be associated with the elite or with a well-equipped scribe, perhaps in government service. From the prismatic finial of a glass stopper retrieved from the same site, one can imagine a finely cut crystal decanter gracing the sideboard of a colonial official's chambers. A metal cuff link bearing the feathers of the Prince of Wales, a decorative pewter button, a gilt walking-stick finial, and an elaborate shoe buckle bring images of well-dressed gentlemen hastening to and from the seat of government. Artifacts often incite visions of people and of small scenes from their daily lives which enhance the more literal documentary accounts. It is this link, the melding of artifacts with the written history of a place, which enables the archeologist to expand and develop the interpretation of broken bits and fragments of culture beyond their simple identification.

While East Florida never achieved a prominant position in colonial trade, ships have managed the difficult bar at St. Augustine for almost four hundred years. British merchants brought their wares to East Florida as early as 1716 when the sloop *Fortune* of Carolina unloaded "European Goods per certificate" in the harbor of St. Augustine.[4] Although illegal, this trade with the Spanish colony existed until 1750 when the Havana Company was compelled to admit English ships without constraint to support its Florida outpost.[5] As a British colony, Florida continued to rely on shipping from Atlantic ports and the British Isles. The creamware services, crystal decanters, London clothing, and large quantities of provisions to support the province all were shipped to St. Augustine to be included in the developing economy of the colony.

When James Grant assumed the governorship of East Florida in 1764, he had a singular mission: populate the new province and develop an economic climate to secure it to the British Empire. He granted huge tracts of land to attract planters and their laborers who would in turn bring artisans, craftsmen, merchants, and traders

3. Hume, *Guide to Artifacts*, p. 191.
4. Joyce E. Harman, *Trade and Privateering in Spanish Florida, 1732–1763* (St. Augustine, 1969), p. 83.
5. Ibid., p. 53.

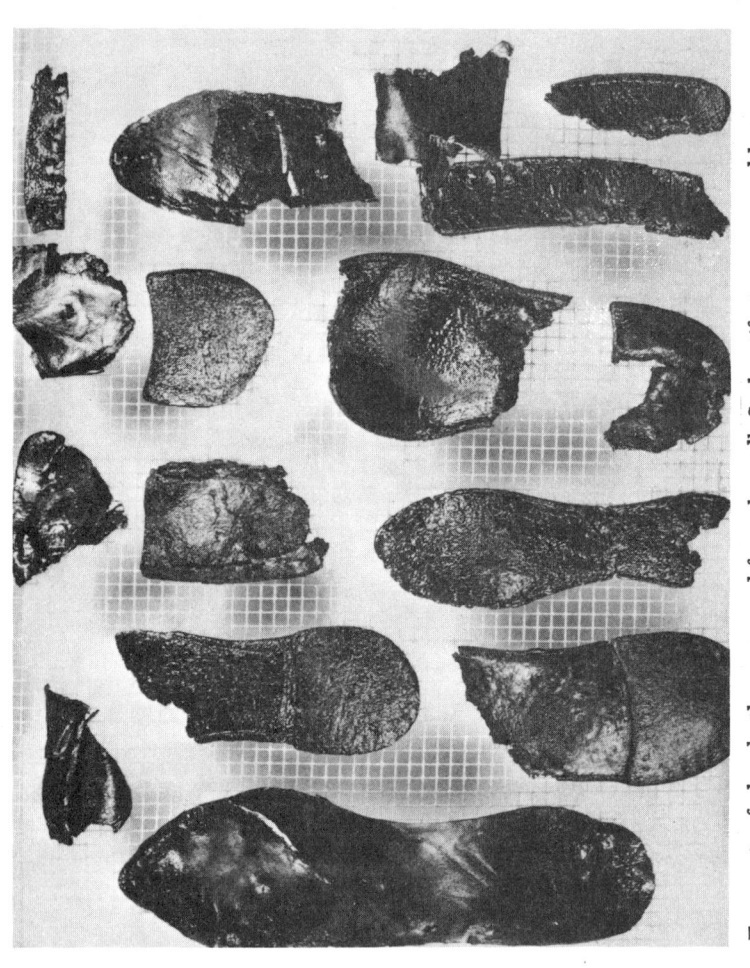

Fragments of shoe leather recovered from the well. Such artifacts are unusual but were preserved in the wet fill of the well. (Historic St. Augustine Preservation Board photo)

Well curb exposed in the 1975 excavations of the plaza well. Concrete from the 1974 Florida Power and Light excavations is seen under the signboard. (Historic St. Augustine Preservation Board photo)

into the colony. He provided a government organization to oversee the colony and soldiers to protect it. Grant created a plantation economy, modeled on those of Virginia and South Carolina, which produced a society into which the bits of glass and ceramics, the rusted iron, and the corroded pewter fit as pieces into a picture puzzle.

Plantation life in Florida must have been arduous in the early years but men like Grant, Moultrie, Richard Oswald, and Jermyn Wright were able to build their agricultural tracts into productive plantations imitating the Georgia style familiar to their countrymen in the other southern colonies. They established an economy based on indigo, rice, lumber, and naval stores and provided food for themselves and the other settlers who came to East Florida.[6] The planters brought indentured whites and enslaved blacks to work in their fields and to tend their stock. An idea of the appearance of these plantations is available from accounts such as John Moultrie's claim to the Crown for losses suffered by the cession: "Bella Vista a plantation on the Matanza River about four Miles from St. Augustine by land of [sic] water, his home and place of residence—a Stone mansion 52 by 42 feet lower Story rustic, upper Ionick, containing a rustic hall 44 feet long. Six arches supports the ceiling; a dining parlour; cov'd drawing room six bed chambers'. two unfinished porticos: Offices and other necessary buildings for a hundred people besides Kitchen garden 10 acres fenced and laid out in pleasure gardens containing a bowling green: laid walks planted with many trees Olives dates oranges lemons limes citrons figs chaddock vines white Mulberry pomegranate peach and plumb banana pines & c. A park in good order about the house off [sic] about 30 acres with many pea fowls. Poland geese Pidgeons, bees & c.—100 acres hard marsh: fish ponds stocked with fresh water fish 300 acres of land well cleared cultivated and well fenced—planted this year 170 acres of corn pease potatoes rice & c.—this plantation contains a thousand acres."[7] Moultrie valued this property at £2,974, and he also owned 100 slaves and 11,836 acres in the province, some of which he had developed for indigo, rice, and turpentine, as well as a residence in St. Augustine.[8]

6. Charles L. Mowat, *East Florida as a British Province, 1763–1784* (Gainesville, Fla., 1964), pp. 69–79.
7. Wilbur Henry Siebert, *Loyalists in East Florida* (DeLand, Fla., 1929), 2:239.
8. Ibid., pp. 240–45.

British Material Culture in St. Augustine / 139

Men like Moultrie gradually increased agricultural production in the colony and acquired wealth to purchase many of the amenities suited to their station.[9] It was the fashion for wealthy British planters in the South to bring furniture, fabric and clothing, and silver and ceramics either directly from England and Scotland or via southern ports rather than rely on New England or mid-Atlantic merchants.[10] Thus, while creamwear, porcelain, cut glass, or pewter cuff links were not the exclusive prerogative of the planter class, the planters were able to bring in quantities of these items and certainly owned the majority of finery in the colony. One well site, of course, cannot be used to demonstrate this conclusively but additional archeological research should be able to test this hypothesis thoroughly.

The planters and their large retinues attracted another strata of society in the many craftsmen, merchants, and innkeepers who found their way into the colony. De Brahm listed almost three hundred free males in East Florida by 1771, and while the majority were planters or farmers, there were ninety-eight employees of the Crown, forty-one storekeepers or innkeepers, seven clothiers, six butchers and bakers, twenty-four carpenters of various sorts, six masonry workers, four shipwrights, two blacksmiths, two barbers, and a goldsmith.[11] The majority must have lived in St. Augustine and plied their trades among the planters, the garrison, and each other.

Each of these men could have contributed artifacts to the community which could eventually have found their way into the well. The innkeepers certainly provided some of the bottles found in the trash. The clothiers provided numerous articles such as buttons, buckles, and a great number of worn-out shoes, and the equally generous butchers added several hundred fragments of bone to the fill. Segments of wood, which survived in the damp soil of the well, and ornamental brasses, common on fine furniture, suggest the woodcrafts; while the recovered plaster, mortar, and bricks certainly passed through a mason's hands. The blacksmiths contributed hundreds of wrought nails, and the goldsmith might have repaired a golden band with two small gold rivets found in the well. Whether

9. Mowat, *East Florida*, p. 153.
10. Alan Gowans, *Images of American Living* (New York, 1964), pp. 178–81.
11. Louis De Vorsey, Jr., *De Brahm's Report of the General Survey of the Southern District of North America* (Columbia, S.C., 1971), pp. 180–86.

or not each of these tradesmen actually did handle any of the material in the well cannot be known. But their role in the community is suggested by the presence of these artifacts.

Historians have already provided glimpses of these tradesmen in documents which tell who they were and what they owned. For example, George Middleton Powell is listed by De Brahm as a storekeeper,[12] and he sought compensation from the Crown for the loss of 2,100 acres, a cooper's shop, 6 horses, a canoe and 4-wheeled wagon, carpenter's tools, a house and lot in St. Augustine and 5,000 shingles.[13] John Wood was a carpenter[14] who owned a lot and several houses in St. Augustine when he sailed to the Bahama Islands in 1783.[15] When and if their houses are located they may reveal much more about what these tradesmen owned and the standard of living they enjoyed as a group.

The British garrison in the colony contributed something of themselves to the well in the plaza. Several large brass buckles associated with cartridge boxes and belts worn during the period by the British infantry came to the surface again after two centuries. Honey-colored French pattern flints, the mainstay of the infantryman in every European army, were recovered as well as two regimental pewter buttons, numbered sixteen and sixty. It is known from documents that both the Sixteenth Regiment of Foot and the Sixtieth, the Royal Americans, were garrisoned in St. Augustine during the Revolution.[16] The military played an increasing role in St. Augustine life as the northern colonies broke with Britain and spread the war to the South, and it would be surprising if military goods were not discovered in the cultural debris of the colony.

There are two groups that, while they are adequately covered in the documentary evidence of the colony, do not appear to be represented by the material culture in the well. The first are the slaves and indentured servants, who comprised the majority of the population in St. Augustine.[17] One might expect, therefore, to find some evidence of their presence in the assemblage recovered from the site. The other group is the native Indian population, and while

12. Ibid., p. 184.
13. Seibert, *Loyalists*, p. 274.
14. De Vorsey, *De Brahm's Report*, p. 186.
15. Siebert, *Loyalists*, p. 268.
16. Mowat, *East Florida*, p. 108.
17. Ibid., p. 64. See De Vorsey, *De Brahm's Report*, for additional population data.

British Material Culture in St. Augustine / 141

there are Indian ceramic sherds in the well they are of the Guale tradition and not associated with the Lower Creek–Seminole groups documented in St. Augustine during the British Period.[18] Only two glass beads indicate that Indians might have been present in St. Augustine.

Thus, creamware and oriental porelain, imported from England, made up over half of the ceramics found in the well. There were large amounts of green glass, primarily representing liquor bottles, and some clear glass from windows, wine glasses, and ornamentals. Elaborate articles associated with clothing and a gold band were found and are associated with wealth and high status. These are all personal artifacts and suggest personal ownership or consumerism. Bottles, buttons, buckles, worn-out shoes, and butchered bones are fragments which suggest products which are bought and sold on a personal level. Wood laths, plaster, mortar, bricks, and nails are architectural in nature and basically represent services which are rendered in concert to produce a building. These artifacts are associated with the tradesmen of the colony, and they represent the production of items which are either personal or architectural, but both are products for the consumer. What about the personal effects of the tradesmen? Large quantities of coarse earthenware were not discovered, and there were no worn-out tools discarded by craftsmen, no cooking utensils, little in the way of broken or discarded hardware or unfinished work, in fact, nothing indicative of the personal artifacts associated with tradesmen. Their domestic-local or shop-local refuse was not deposited in the well. The soldiers left items peculiar to that vocation to indicate their presence, but they were not involved in activities which would cause them to lose any quantity of their specialized equipment near the well. Slaves and the indentured servants left nothing, nor did the Indians.

From the artifacts that were recovered and from those that were absent, several alternate deductions may be attempted which relate to social interaction at this site. First, it can be assumed that the plaza well was not a representative site for the social interaction in East Florida since there is an inverse proportion of material evidence associated with documented groups in the province. The archeological evidence contradicts the documentation. The numer-

18. The Guale tribes left with the Spanish in 1763, and the presence of these sherds indicates that they became mixed with British middens, a common occurrence in St. Augustine archeology.

ically larger group—slaves, indentured servants, and Indians—are not represented at all, while the minority planter group appears to be represented by great quantities of artifacts. If this single site was representative, one would expect the opposite findings.

The plaza well is in fact not representative of the population of East Florida. It would be presumptuous to expect one site to provide that quantity of information. The well was situated on the plaza between the house of the governor of East Florida and the state house. It was filled with refuse from middens presumably associated with these buildings and the people who frequented them. The recovered material represents the tastes and economic position of the planter and official class in East Florida. Men of means and influence traveled to this location to conduct their most important business and the setting must have complemented the situation.

The material recovered from this site also provides a glimpse of the interaction between the planters and officials and the merchants and craftsmen. These groups were attracted to the province initially to support the planter economy, and the glass, bone, clothing items, and construction materials indicate they were indeed providing these services to the elite minority.

The well debris offers few clues about other groups in East Florida. It will be necessary to locate and excavate additional sites in order to illuminate their life-styles. Perhaps Moultrie's Bella Vista, when it is discovered, will provide a picture of plantation life and how indentured servants and slaves lived their ordinary lives. The exploration of George Middleton Powell's or John Wood's properties may provide evidence of the domestic side of their lives, and an Indian campsite would certainly advance our scant knowledge of this group in East Florida. Perhaps when work of this kind is completed we will have a much clearer understanding of the inhabitants of East Florida as subjects of the British Crown.

What Our Southern Frontier Women Wore

ANNA C. EBERLY

WHAT women of fashion wore in the early South has already been well documented. What has not been so extensively researched has been the types of clothing and the mode of dress of the women of the lower and middle classes in the southern colonies before and at the time of the American Revolution. The basic components of eighteenth-century female dress—shifts, petticoats, bodices—were similar throughout the South, particularly among women who worked in the home and in the fields. The only differences were due to specific working situations, climate, availability of goods, and/or the ethnic background of the women involved.

Doing research for this kind of project is sometimes difficult. One can get examples of different articles of clothing, but there is not much information on how these pieces were worn. Valuable sources of information were contemporary newspaper advertisements offering rewards for runaway servants who had left without fulfilling their contracts or for escaped slaves. These advertisements often supplied both physical details of the person and the kind of clothing worn at the time of the escape. The major problem here was the fact that the escapees, whether servants or slaves, were usually wearing everything they owned. Sometimes they were wearing garments that belonged to someone else, clothing which they had stolen. In the *Virginia Gazette* of March 1774, there was an advertisement for a runaway Negro woman, who was wearing, or at least carrying, a striped holland weskit (a waistcoat), Virginia-cloth petticoat, osnaburg shift, Virginia-cloth gown, white dimity and striped Virginia-cloth petticoat, an osnaburg shirt, and other stuffs. Obviously she was not wearing all of these garments at one time. Presumably she was carrying some items in a pack. It reveals, however, the types of clothing that she had access to, whether or not they actually belonged to her. In a Maryland paper of January 4, 1770, there was a description of Annie Hand, a runaway black, who was wearing a dark colored wool dress, a red petticoat, and a black silk hat.

Wills and inventories supply information about contemporary clothing and their relative values. Many colonies, and later the states, required precise inventories to be compiled when the head of a household died. From these lists much can be learned about the value of clothing, and perhaps even more important, how much clothing the deceased person owned. Economic status would have much to do with the size and quality of an individual's wardrobe. From account books kept by seamstresses and tailors there are data on the amount, type, and cost of fabrics used in making different garments, and whether they were made locally or imported from Europe. Archeological finds have revealed buttons, shreds of fabric, buckles, and other clothing details which are valuable source items. Original articles of clothing are vital resources. More often the clothing that has survived is part of museum collections and was worn by the upper classes. Survival itself suggests that they were of better quality to begin with. If these garments do not reveal what was worn by southern working-class females, they do supply important details as to their method of construction, which was very different from twentieth-century clothing. Tailors' pattern books, fashion dolls of the period, English women's magazines (one was being printed in London in 1774) all reveal something about clothing, from style to the kinds of embroidery, buttons, and thread that were used. Other information is available from contemporary literature—the novels of Fielding and Smollett—and the plays of the period. Travel accounts are rich sources, and it is fortunate that there are some which relate to the southern colonies during the eighteenth century. The Reverend James Woodmason, an itinerant Anglican minister, describing a congregaton near Rocky Mount, North Carolina, said, "The men with only a thin shirt and a pair of britches or trousers on, bare-legged, and barefooted. The women bare-headed and bare-legged, and bare-foot with only a thin shift and under petticoat. Yet I can not break them of this, for the heat of the weather admits not any but thin clothing. I can hardly bear the weight of my wig and gown during the services." He was a fairly intolerant gentleman, and apparently he did not really approve of the people.

The *Journal of a Lady of Quality* was written by a Scotswoman who was in the Wilmington, North Carolina, area during 1775, in the period just before the American Revolution. Although she was contemptuous of the lowly settlers, her *Journal* is one of the most astute commentaries on the social life in the eighteenth-century South. Describing what people were wearing and using she wrote, "The heat increases daily, as do the mosquitoes, the bugs and the ticks. The curtains of our beds are now supplied by mosquitoes nets. Fannie has got a new, rather elegant dressing room, the settees of which are canopied over with green gauze and on these we lie panting for breath and air, dressed in a single muslin petticoat and a short gown."

The most common clothing fabrics were linen, wool, cotton, or a combination of these. There were a variety of weights and qualities of linen. Lawn was a very fine, almost transparent linen. Holland was a shirting white linen. Ticking was a striped, medium-weight linen used very often in men's trousers and in women's petticoats. Both dowlas and osnaburg were heavy fabrics. Virginia cloth is mentioned very frequently in the notices and advertisements in the *Virginia Gazette* and in the *Maryland Gazette*. It was likely a heavy fabric, a combination of linen and cotton, that was popular in making clothing for the servants and laborers. The cottons were calico, chintz, and dimity. The wools were broadcloth, flannel, melton, and linsey-woolsey. This latter was a coarse, sturdy fabric with a cotton warp and a woolen filling; the warp gave it strength. It was used often in the eighteenth century. There were, of course, beautiful silks, velvets, brocades, and other rich fabrics for those who could afford such expensive material to fashion into gowns.

There was a variety of colors—red, blue, yellow, gold, brown, green, and any combination of these—which could be achieved by mineral and vegetable dyes. Yellow was a very popular color of the times. Stripes and checks were often used. Printed linens and cottons were available, and in the colonies where the population was predominantly Spanish (this was true of Florida before 1763) probably there were also painted linens. Trailing-flowers in the Chinese manner were sometimes used on chintz and floral stripes were very popular. There was a fabric which had a solid-color warp with a weft of two different threads woven as one, which gave it a tweedy effect.

A popular article of clothing of the period was the shift or chemise. It was a voluminous garment reaching midcalf or longer, with a low decolleté, which could be adjusted with a drawstring casing. The sleeve was gathered or pleated on to a drop shoulder, ending at a ruffle at the elbow. Women of means might have embroidered trebled sleeve ruffles made out of lawn, sometimes with lace attached. This was the most intimate eighteenth-century female garment because under this the lady wore nothing at all. Underclothing as they are known in the twentieth century did not exist for the eighteenth-century woman, but the shift or chemise functioned almost as a twentieth-century combination of a slip, blouse, and nightgown. The front of this garment was usually low, and the back high. Spanish women also wore shifts although the sleeves were a bit longer and were rolled above the elbow and tied with a ribbon.

The petticoat in the eighteenth century was the garment that women now call the skirt. A "skirt" at that time, however, as an item worn by females, referred to a garment that had been adapted from men's attire. For instance, the riding habit was basically a man's garment. When a woman wore such an outfit, she might refer to the skirts of a riding habit. Eighteenth-century skirts referred to the lower portion of the weskit or coat worn by men.

The petticoat was worn at different lengths depending upon the woman's station in life and the kind of work she performed. Women of the upper class, those who could afford servants, could wear long petticoats; since someone else was likely to be doing the cooking, they did not have to worry about dragging their garments in the fireplace. The petticoat, like the twentieth-century skirt, was fastened at the waist by a drawstring but some were pleated or gathered onto a waistband. The length of this garment could be adjusted by the use of a loop and button. The woman could also tuck part of the garment into her waistband when she was working. Petticoats were not underwear, although sometimes a petticoat was worn underneath an outer petticoat. If it was worn in this manner it was called an under petticoat.

The apron was another article of absolute necessity for the working woman in the eighteenth century. It was worn to protect the petticoat, but it might also be used as a hot pad or as a dish rag, for example. The work aprons were very long, usually only an inch or two above the bottom of the petticoat, and they were very full to make the best use of the garment. They could be pulled up and tucked into the waist to provide a large pocket. The wearer might flip it to the side and then tuck it in to keep the frontside of the apron clean. It could be used to carry wood or vegetables. It might have a pocket sewn on it. Aprons were also made with a drawstring waist or with a waistband with ties. The pinner apron had a bib attached to the waist and was pinned to the shift or bodice. Women of fashion also wore aprons. They might be scalloped along the edges; they were probably made out of lawn and perhaps embroidered. These aprons were very fancy articles of fashion and obviously not designed to be worn while working.

The bodices of the eighteenth century—jacket bodices, waistcoats, stays—all provided basic support for the body. The brassiere as it is known today did not exist in this early period. Women used the bodice to support their busts. Bodices were cut low and wide to provide support, and those with slightly boned or unboned stays were called jumps. Stays in the eighteenth century were very confining garments, very difficult, if not impossible, to work in. They were fastened with ties, lacings, or hooks and eyes. Bodices had to be very tight or they would not function properly and would ride up. Stays were very rigid in construction. They were sleeveless and cut low to provide support. In examining a detail from a French staymaker's pattern book, one notes that all of the lines are whalebones. There was also a pocket in the front of the stays where one could insert what was called a busk. This might be bone or it might be wood, but it kept one's posture erect. It also made it impossible to do a lot of bending over but could be removed at will.

The over gown was also called a short gown. It reached to about the knees and was probably worn with some type of supporting garment underneath, because it was not tight fitting. Stays or perhaps half-bone stays were used for support.

The kerchief was worn as an article of fashion, but it was also a very practical garment. When one went outside it was used to protect the bosom from sun, wind, or the cold. It was a square or triangular piece of fabric that would be folded and thrown about the shoulders and tucked into the bodice. A woman of fashion would wear one made of very fine lawn, perhaps embroidered, or scalloped, and it might possibly be fastened with a brooch at the bosom.

The pelerine was a triangle of fabric that was worn for warmth. It was placed about the shoulders like the kerchief, but tied in the back providing a minimum amount of warmth, while leaving the arms free to work. Also there were scarves which were rounded in the back and had the lappets or the long section hanging down in the front but were not tied. They were very often decorated with scallops, ruching of fabric, or lace. Scarves were mostly wool, although they could be more decorative and fashioned of silk or velvet fabrics for ladies of the upper classes. They were made just like the linen kerchief only much larger in size.

Cloaks were worn throughout the eighteenth century. They were full, and gathered and fastened at the neckline. Many were made with attached hoods, with a drawstring in the hood to keep it from blowing off. The cardinal cloak was patterned after the church garment and red was a favorite color.

Head coverings of the eighteenth century were incredibly varied. In a book published in London in 1725 some 250 ways to dress the head are shown. Head scarves were also worn by the Spanish women, but the ends were not tied in the back and they were called *mantillas*. Women wore caps both in and out of doors. It was rare for a woman not to utilize a head covering in the eighteenth century. Small mob caps were worn indoors. Overcaps, the outside headgear, were worn on top of the inside caps. While riding, a woman wore a cocked hat, which was originally a man's item of attire. Straw hats, adapted for use by the upper classes from the lower classes, were common throughout the last half of the eighteenth century. Working women had needed these to protect them from the sun when they were laboring outdoors.

Pockets were tied about the waist and were worn underneath or on top of the petticoat. They had a slit down the front to provide access to the inside. Sometimes there were slits in the skirt to reach an inner pocket.

The stockings of the eighteenth century were knitted thread stockings—cotton worsted or silk—sometimes with replaceable feet. Stockings reached above the knee, and were tied either above or below the knee with garters, strips of fabric or ribbon which might be decorated with sayings or mottoes.

Shoes were heeled, with buckles or with ties which fastened over the central tongue. They were usually made of leather for the lower classes, while cloth slippers were worn by affluent ladies. In the earlier part of the century heels were higher, becoming lower and much broader by the 1770s. Clogs were worn throughout the century by the poorer classes. Patents were overshoes and according to one contemporary description, "The women leave in the passage their patents. That is a kind of wooden shoes which stand on a high iron ring. Into these wooden shoes they thrust their ordinary leather or stuff shoes when they go out."

Cosmetics, or makeup, were not very common for women of the lower classes in the eighteenth century. Women of fashion, however, used red and white paint on their lips and fingernails. They tweezed their eyebrows, darkened them, and sometimes shaved them off completely and replaced them with strips of moleskin. They had patches made of silk or black velvet which they glued onto their face or their bosom. They had many perfumes, creams, and lotions which helped mask their odors, since they could seldom bathe.

The fashionable women of the eighteenth century have been well described and their clothing from this early period survives in museums all over the world. Women of the lower and middle classes also had a sense of fashion, even though they lived and worked under what must have been difficult circumstances, bearing many children, keeping up large households, and sometimes following their men off to war. Yet even if they lacked access to money and thus to the fashions of Europe, many still managed to maintain their femininity and their sense of style.

BICENTENNIAL COMMISSION
OF FLORIDA

Governor Reubin O'D. Askew, *Honorary Chairman*
Lieutenant Governor J. H. Williams, *Chairman*
Harold W. Stayman, Jr., *Vice Chairman*
William R. Adams, *Executive Director*

Dick J. Batchelor, Orlando
Johnnie Ruth Clarke, St. Petersburg
A. H. "Gus" Craig, St. Augustine
James J. Gardener, Fort Lauderdale
Jim Glisson, Tavares
Mattox Hair, Jacksonville
Thomas L. Hazouri, Jacksonville
Ney C. Landrum, Tallahassee
Mrs. Raymond Mason, Jacksonville
Carl C. Mertins, Jr., Pensacola
Charles E. Perry, Miami
W. E. Potter, Orlando
F. Blair Reeves, Gainesville
Richard R. Renick, Coral Gables
Jane W. Robinson, Cocoa
Mrs. Robert L. Shevin, Tallahassee
Don Shoemaker, Miami
Mary L. Singleton, Jacksonville
Bruce A. Smathers, Tallahassee
Alan Trask, Fort Meade
Edward J. Trombetta, Tallahassee
Ralph D. Turlington, Tallahassee
William S. Turnbull, Orlando
Robert Williams, Tallahassee
Lori Wilson, Merritt Island